MASTER
it
FASTER

MASTER
it
FASTER

by

Colin Rose

First published January 1999
by Accelerated Learning Systems Ltd

First published by The Industrial Society in 2000
The Industrial Society
Robert Hyde House
48 Bryanston Square
London W1H 2EA
Telephone: +44 (0)20 7479 2000

© Colin Rose, 2000

ISBN 1 85835 806 X

Industrial Society
Business Books Network
163 Central Avenue
Suite 2, Hopkins Professional Building
Dover, NH 03820
USA

British Library Cataloguing-in-Publication Data
A catalogue record for this book is available from the British Library.

Library of Congress
Cataloguing-in-Publication
Data on File.

Printed by: J W Arrowsmith Ltd
Typeset by: The Midlands Book Typesetting Company
Cover image by: Digital Vision
Cover design by: Sign
The Industrial Society is a Registered Charity No. 290003

COLIN ROSE

Colin Rose wrote the original book *Accelerated Learning* in 1983 and founded Accelerated Learning Systems Ltd in 1984. In 1996 he co-wrote *Accelerated Learning in the 21st Century,* to include the latest research into learning styles and new ways of learning. The M.A.S.T.E.R model for learning has grown out of this research.

He has consulted with major international organizations on innovative methods of learning and training and has spoken at many international educational and training conferences.

The M.A.S.T.E.R model explored in this book has been used to design and develop self-study foreign language courses in French, German, Spanish and Italian, and Japanese for English speakers – in conventional tape, video and book form and also in CD-ROM format. It has been used to design and develop a Training and Development Programme for corporate and organizational trainers.

He has also developed and co-written a Pre-School Development Programme for parents called FUNdamentals.

He is a Member of The Royal Society of Arts and was on the original steering committee for the RSA's national initiative *The Campaign for Learning.*

ACKNOWLEDGEMENTS

This book has evolved from my research into how people learn and why some fail yet others succeed in developing their full potential.

It is impossible to acknowledge all the authors, educators and trainers whose thoughts and ideas have influenced my own. I would, at least, like to mention and thank the following. Some are now friends, some I have only met through their writings.

John Abbott, Dr Thomas Armstrong, Sir Christopher Ball, Chris Brewer, Tony Buzan, Don Campbell, Dr Arthur Costa, Dr Mihaly Csikzentmihalyi, Edward De Bono, Bobbi DePorter, Dr Lynn Dhority, Dr Marian Diamond, Dee Dickinson, Gordon Dryden, Dr Robert Fisher, Dr Howard Gardner, Mary Jane Gill, Philip Goldberg, Daniel Goleman, John Grinder, Michael Grinder, Sir Charles Handy, Leslie Hart, Dr Jane Healy, Dr Jean Houston, Eric Jensen, David and Roger Johnson, Kristina Kleist, Peter Kline, Dr Georgi Lozanov, Dr Luiz Machado, Dr Paul Maclean, Rollo May, Dr Paul Messier, George Miller, Robert Ornstein, Dr Lyelle Palmer, Sidney Parnes, Dr Richard Paul, Dr David Perkins, Robert Pike, Carl Rogers, Bob Samples, Dr Don Schuster, Ted Sizer, Dr Roger Sperry, Dr Robert Sternberg, Dr Robert Sylwester, Daniel Tobin, Dr James Tooley, Brian Tracy, Dr Jeannette Vos, Dr Win Wenger, Arthur Whimbey.

CONTENTS

Three Skills you Need

To be able to learn fast, make good decisions and think creatively are amongst the most important skills anyone can acquire. For three reasons:

- **Information is coming at us at an accelerating rate.**
- **Jobs are changing faster and faster.**
- **Society, work and even leisure pursuits are becoming more complex.**

The accelerating pace of information means that you need to know how to absorb information more rapidly. Information is doubling every four years.

Faster change means that you and the organization you work for must learn and adapt more quickly. The job you are doing now is unlikely to be the same job that you will be doing in even three years' time.

Increased complexity means that the ability to analyze situations logically and to solve problems creatively are skills that **everyone** needs in their work – and indeed private life.

The competitive edge

It's no longer enough to have these skills just at the top of an organization. The companies which will succeed are those who trust their people to make quality decisions on the spot. There simply isn't time to wait for 'someone else' to decide everything.

In other words, the individuals and companies who can out-learn, out-think and out-create their competitors will be the ones who will thrive in the 21st century.

In an increasingly unsure world, the more successful the organization that you work for, the more secure your job is. And successful companies are becoming what has been termed 'learning organizations'.

Learning organizations set out to ensure that every ounce of the knowledge and intelligence possessed by their staff is focused on achieving aims that everyone has agreed to.

WE HAVE TO KEEP UP!

Companies and individuals who are not continuously learning – new skills and new information – are falling behind those who are.

Learning is the competitive edge for the 21st century.

Your earning power depends on your learning power.

"The only truly educated person is the one who has learned how to learn."

Carl Rogers
Educational psychologist

In a learning organization you don't wait to be trained. You decide what it is you need to learn to succeed in your job (and in your personal life) and simply go ahead and learn it. 'Top down training' is replaced with 'bottom up learning'.

For that to happen means that everyone needs to be good at learning fast, skilled at analyzing situations systematically and good at coming up with creative solutions to problems.

Plugging a gap

The problem is that it's rare for even a highly educated person to have been taught the techniques of learning effectively and thinking analytically or creatively. It is a major gap in our educational system.

We get taught what – but not how. Yet fast learning and clear thinking are both skills that can be learned and taught. They are skills that increase your own 'market value' and increase your 'employability' in the fast-changing world of work.

And anyone who can teach learning and thinking skills has an invaluable gift to pass on to their family.

What we've learned about learning

More has been discovered about the human brain in the last 15 - 20 years than in all previous history. It allows us to say that each person's brain is as individual as their fingerprints.

That uniqueness means that each person has a personal learning style – a way of learning that suits them best. You too.

> When you learn the techniques that best match your preferred learning style, you will be learning in the way that is most natural to you.
>
> Because it's natural (brain friendly) – it's easier. Because it's easier, it's quicker. That's why it's called Accelerated Learning.

Yet although everyone has an individual learning style, there are common steps everyone needs to take to learn effectively.

A journey can have a common start point and the same end point, yet offer a wide choice of paths in between.

So, whilst this programme offers a single framework for effective learning it also allows for large variations in individual learning styles.

A KEY SKILL

What you know today won't guarantee success tomorrow. It may well be out of date!

Since lifelong learning is the key to success, knowing **how** to learn effectively is a fundamental skill.

CREATIVITY

Getting enough information these days isn't difficult. We're swamped with it.

The secret of success is to use the information that everyone else has, to create new ideas that no one else thought of.

What's in this book

The first part of the book examines how you learn. Then it describes learning techniques that match the way your brain likes to learn best – in order to speed up your learning.

You will be invited to consider the significance of the ideas:

1   As a learner yourself.

2   As someone who might need to train and help others learn.

3   As an adult who may well need to help a child to learn effectively.

Some of the subjects we will cover include:

- How to triple your reading speed.

- 14 strategies for a better memory.

- The eight human intelligences. Why that means each person has a personal learning style and how you can use this knowledge to learn better and become a more effective communicator.

- How to develop a near photographic memory for names.

- The six rules of persuasive writing.

- How to think for new ideas.

- How to work smarter not harder.

Work is shifting from manpower to mindpower.

EVERYONE'S A TEACHER

More and more training is being done by people who know the subject well but are not professional trainers.

So this book contains some proven ways to help you help others learn.

Assets used to be measured in cash, machinery and land.

The new riches are based on ideas and knowledge.

"Each of us guards a gate of change that can only be opened from inside".

Marilyn Ferguson

You've Got What it Takes!

What we've learned about the human brain in the last 15 years should have revolutionized education and training. But it hasn't yet! Which is why this book can make such a significant contribution to you and your family.

A human brain is an incredibly complex and capable piece of equipment – but it comes without an owner's manual. It is rather like having a super-computer, but without all the programs to make it work properly.

ARE YOU BEING ACTIVE OR PASSIVE?

Active learners will be reading this with a pencil in their hand. Ready to jot down questions and conclusions.

Three brains in one

We actually have three brains. Each one evolved after the other.

At the base of your skull you have a rather primitive brain. It keeps you breathing and it keeps your heart beating. It tells you to fight or run when danger threatens. It also controls some of your more primitive instincts, like your sense of territory. So you feel angry or uncomfortable when someone moves too close to you.

PRIMITIVE OR REPTILIAN BRAIN

Next to evolve was your middle brain or limbic system, a type of brain that mammals also possess.

Your middle brain controls your hormonal system, your health (immune system), your sexuality, emotions and an important part of your long-term memory.

MIDDLE BRAIN OR LIMBIC SYSTEM

The fact that our emotions and our long-term memory are **both** controlled from this same middle brain explains why, when something involves strong emotions, it is usually very well remembered. You probably remember your first kiss, for example? Or where you were when you heard someone significant had died. It also means enjoyment and fun are important elements in learning, because they involve positive emotions.

Make a fist with your hand. Now wrap your other hand over the top of this fist. If your wrist represents your primitive brain, and the fist is your middle brain, the hand wrapped over it represents your new brain or neo-cortex.

This third brain is truly extraordinary. It has **all** the capacity you will ever need to learn and remember anything you want. So long as you know how!

NEO-CORTEX OR THINKING BRAIN

As it grows in the womb, a 12-week-old human embryo is developing about 2,000 brain cells a second.

An adult bee – which can do some pretty sophisticated things like building a honeycomb, calculating distances, and signalling the direction of pollen to its companions – has a total of about 7,000 brain cells or neurons.

That's the number of brain cells that a human embryo grows in about three seconds!

USE IT OR LOSE IT!

Some sounds in a foreign language are difficult to master in later life. That's because you don't hear them or use them in your native language. So the brain connections are lost.

It's called 'neural pruning'.

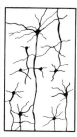

PARENTS TAKE NOTE

Some 50% of a child's physical brain capacity is built in the first five years of life.

That's why it's important to create a stimulating, rich environment for your child without falling into the trap of becoming a 'hot-house' parent.

Building your own brain

The incredible capacity of the brain has only recently been realized. You have about 100 **billion** brain cells. A number that is almost impossible to visualize. It's 20 times the entire population of the world.

A brain cell looks a bit like a miniature octopus. The cell is in the middle. Branching out from it are tiny threads. Each time something reaches one of your senses (eg: sight, sound, or touch), it creates a thought or impression that travels out from a brain cell and along one of the little branch-like threads. (These threads are called 'dendrites' from a Greek word meaning branch.)

A BRAIN CELL

Then the thought crosses over to another brain cell, via its 'branch'. The process continues with perhaps thousands or millions of brain cells being connected up in sequence. A split second mental chain reaction conducted by electrical activity.

Each time this chain reaction takes place, new connections are formed between brain cells. Some of these connections become permanent with repetition. That is why you can remember so many things without conscious effort, like riding a bike.

TWO BRAIN CELLS CONNECTING

Here is the significance. It is not really the number of brain cells you have, it is the number of **connections** you make between those brain cells that determines how 'useful' your brain becomes, ie: how intelligent you are.

The conclusion from brain scientists over the last 10 - 15 years is that intelligence is not fixed. Because the more you use your brain, the more connections you make between your brain cells. The more connections between your brain cells, the greater is your potential for intelligent thought.

SECTION OF A STIMULATED BRAIN

SECTION OF AN UNSTIMULATED BRAIN

You literally expand your brain through use. You are the architect of your own brain. You can develop your own intelligence by stimulating your mind.

Old age is no handicap

Barring injury or major illness, you do not lose brain capacity as you grow older, as long as you keep learning and keep seeking new experiences – through hobbies, reading, work, sports, art, music, etc.

More about the thinking brain

Imagine you are looking down on top of your head and are able to see through your skull to the thinking brain within. What you would see is that the top thinking brain (or neo-cortex) consists of two distinct halves. The two halves are connected by a rich bundle of nerves, called the Corpus Callosum.

Ingenious research suggests that each half of the brain tends to have its own style of processing information for learning.

LEFT BRAIN SPECIALITIES
  Speech
  Step-by-step logic
  Numbers

RIGHT BRAIN SPECIALITIES
  Melody
  Patterns
  Intuition

It's important not to exaggerate the difference between the left and right brain because our brains are far too complex to be put into neat categories. Nevertheless, there is an important conclusion from this research. Some people prefer a slow step-by-step build up of information. We call them the more 'linear' type of learner.

Others prefer – indeed need – to see the 'big picture' of the subject. An initial overview so they can see where it all leads to. (It's difficult to do a jigsaw without the picture on the box in front of you!) We call them the more 'global' type of learner.

When we listen to a song, the left brain will basically be attending to the words, the right brain will be attending to the melody. In addition, the emotional centre of your brain, or limbic system, will be engaged. **In other words your whole brain is actively involved.**

Now think how comparatively easy it is to learn the words of a song. You probably know dozens, maybe hundreds of songs – yet you normally make little conscious effort to learn them.

> ### USE IT OR LOSE IT!
>
> The brain thrives on novelty, and only declines with lack of stimulation.

> "The brain may well be like a miracle computer. But it's also the only one that runs on glucose, generates 10 watts of electricity and is created by unskilled labour!"
>
> **David Lewis**

> ### KEEP ACTIVE!
>
> Are you asking questions as you read?
>
> A question you might ask right now is … "Am I more of a Linear or Global learner?"

> "In a rapidly changing environment, people will need to move in and out of education all their lives."
>
> **Professor Tom Stonier**
> Bradford University

ACTION

Take a few moments to think about what you have just read. The conditions under which you listen to a song are usually relaxed and stress free. What does this information tell you about the conditions for effective learning?

Does it make sense to combine activities that involve the whole brain as we learn? Combine, for example, pictures and words? Or words and music? Or the overall big picture with detail?

TEACHING STYLE MUST MATCH LEARNING STYLE

Learning styles and teaching styles need to be matched to enable learning to be enjoyable and successful.

STYLES

The style of teaching that used to characterize our educational system was typically "sit still, face the front, and listen to me".

That style of teaching suits less than half the population.

No wonder so many people feel they could have done better at school than they did. And that feeling still affects their attitude to learning years later.

Dr Benjamin Bloom has spent a lifetime studying excellence.

His conclusion is that anyone can learn anything – the only difference is that some take more time than others.

A very simplified way to explain the difference between 'linear' and 'global' thinking would be to imagine meeting someone you know.

A totally 'linear' approach would be to scan the hair, the forehead, then the eyebrows, the eyes, nose, mouth and chin. It is a slow, logical, step-by-step build-up of information in sequence.

Of course we don't do that. We glance at the person and instantly our right-brain capacity for global thinking means we see the **pattern.** The result is we recognize the person.

Most traditional educational materials rely too heavily on a linear presentation, ie: a slow, detailed build up of information. The more global learners get frustrated. They cannot see where it's all leading to. So they get bored and switch off.

Most of our learning experiences have tended to be based on the type of instruction that linear learners like. So for people who like intuitive thinking, school rarely enables them to achieve their full potential. But those who rely more on a linear type of thinking miss out too – they have not been given the chance to develop more creative styles of thinking.

Change from linear to global

Absolutely stuck with something new you are learning? Unable to retain it? Unable to maintain interest and concentration while you read?

Look at the way you are approaching it. Can you identify your approach as linear or global? For example, if you are laboriously working your way through a text book taking careful notes – try something radically different. Try using some visual images – take a range of coloured pens and create a poster that represents what you are trying to learn. You will have changed from a linear approach to a more whole-brain mode of learning.

Emotions and learning

Information entering our brain will travel to the middle brain. The middle brain acts as a sort of central switchboard. If it decides the information is worthwhile, it switches that information up to your 'thinking brain'.

Now remember that this middle brain is not only a 'switchboard', it is also the part of your brain that controls your emotions. So, when the new information is transmitted to you in ways that appeal positively to your emotions, you can learn well and remember well.

When what we are learning includes colour, illustrations, games and sometimes a musical accompaniment, our emotions are engaged positively, and we learn better.

Which teachers do you remember from school? Chances are the ones who were enthusiastic. Enthusiasm has emotional appeal.

However, when negative emotions or fear are present, the middle brain may suppress the incoming information.

If you are under stress, information may never even reach your thinking brain. It gets filtered out. That is what happens when someone's mind goes blank. They have 'down-shifted' to a more primitive way of thinking.

Stress, however, is not only the worry and concerns that you are conscious of. Often people with a poor previous experience of learning are unconsciously threatened by new learning experiences.

It becomes a vicious circle. Because they feel they are poor at learning, they feel threatened. And because they feel under threat their neo-cortex receives less information, so they do learn less effectively!

If you feel insecure, less of your brain's potential is available. That is why, when you are worried, you may suddenly come to realize that you have been staring at a page, without taking anything in. That's why your state of mind is so important in learning.

STRESSED   RELAXED

The secret is to get into a calm positive mood, **before** you start to learn.

You have eight intelligences to use

Almost everyone has the brain capacity to be an efficient learner. With 100 **billion** brain cells, you'd have to be downright greedy to want any more! But how do we actually use our brain to learn? Why do most of us use only a fraction of its potential? And what is intelligence?

Work by Dr Howard Gardner, who is Professor of Education at Harvard University, points to the fact that we have not just 'an' intelligence – but at least seven, possibly eight. Possibly a lot more. Each intelligence is of **similar** importance in reaching our full human potential.

Let's look at those eight different intelligences. We can recognize them as natural talents, which each of us has to a greater or lesser extent.

STRESSED OR STRETCHED?

There is a difference between stress, which is negative, and the feeling of tension you get before you start something that you know will stretch your ability.

We feel good when we rise to a challenge. A game with an opponent with whom we need to struggle to win. Mastering a new skill at work.

To be stretched is positive – it makes life fun. Chicago University psychologist, Mihaly Csikzentmihalyi, calls the excitement of being stretched "a state of flow – where you are so involved that nothing else seems to matter".

DON'T UNDERESTIMATE THE IMPORTANCE OF INDIVIDUALITY

Tests show that simply shifting a book to the left or right of the body can improve some people's reading speed and understanding!

1   **Linguistic Intelligence** – or talent with language

The ability to write or talk fluently. Some people just seem to have the 'gift of the gab' – they can write well, and read well. They have good linguistic intelligence.

Famous examples:
Winston Churchill, Shakespeare, Wordsworth, Abraham Lincoln, Goethe, Molière

2   **Mathematical/Logical Intelligence** – or talent with maths, logic and systems

The ability to deal well with numbers and to think logically. You probably know people who perhaps do not think of themselves as 'intelligent', but who are razor sharp in adding up the odds on a bet, or at calculating statistics for football or baseball!

Engineers, scientists and accountants would demonstrate this intelligence.

Famous examples:
Einstein, Stephen Hawking, Isaac Newton

3   **Visual/Spatial Intelligence** – or visual talent

The ability to visualize how things will eventually look. To imagine things in your mind's eye.

Designers, architects and artists would be an example, but **you** use it when you use your sense of direction, navigate or draw well.

Famous examples:
Picasso, Christopher Columbus, Frank Lloyd Wright

4   **Musical Intelligence** – or talent with music

The ability to create and interpret music. To keep rhythm. Many of us have a good basic musical intelligence and we can all develop it. Think how helpful it is to learn with a jingle or rhyme (eg: 30 days hath September).

Famous examples:
Mozart,
Leonard Bernstein,
Louis Armstrong

5   **Bodily/Physical Intelligence**

You use this intelligence when you move well, run, dance, build and construct something. All arts and crafts use this intelligence.

Many people who are physically talented and 'good with their hands' do not recognize that they are showing a high form of intelligence. One that is of **equal value** to the other intelligences.

Famous examples:
Pelé,
Margot Fonteyn,
Charlie Chaplin

6   **Inter-personal Intelligence** – or social talent

The ability to communicate well and get on with others. Many people have a superb ability to make people feel at ease, to read others' reactions and to be sympathetic to the feelings of others.

This is a vital human intelligence. This talent is used to the full in being a good parent, politician, leader, a supportive colleague or a good teacher.

Famous examples:
Martin Luther King,
Mother Teresa,
J F Kennedy

7   **Intra-personal Intelligence** – or inner control

An ability for quiet, objective, self-analysis. This leads to being able to understand your own behaviour and feelings.

You use this intelligence to create your own goals and plans, and to study your own successes and mistakes as a guide to future improvement.

Famous examples:
Socrates, Freud,
Bertrand Russell

8   **Naturalist Intelligence**

The ability to recognize elements in the natural world, live in harmony with it and use it productively. Farmers, botanists, biologists and environmentalists display this intelligence.

Famous examples:
Charles Darwin,
David Attenborough,
E O Wilson

It is worth spending a few minutes looking at this list of eight intelligences or talents again. **Be aware that they are of equal value**.

This new way of looking at people's ability has led Dr Howard Gardner to propose a new definition of 'intelligence'. It is "the ability to create useful products and solve everyday problems".

Previously, intelligence was defined much more narrowly. It was measured mostly by I.Q. tests that concentrated on linguistic and mathematical/logical intelligence. So it was quite good at predicting academic performance because academic subjects are largely taught through the linguistic and mathematical/logical intelligences.

Academic success is indeed one way of demonstrating intelligence. In the real world, however, it is **far** from the only way. What's more, when teaching or training involves a wider range of intelligences it opens up many more opportunities for many more people.

To paraphrase Howard Gardner "Multiple intelligence learning = multiple chance education".

Conclusion

To all intents and purposes the basic capacity of a human brain is limitless. Most people, however, use only a fraction of their true potential, for three reasons:

1   They lack self-confidence.

2   They lack an organized approach to learning.

3   They do not know how to use their preferred learning style and their full range of intelligences.

Active learning

As you read through the rest of this book, why not stop frequently and ask yourself these three questions:

• Can I use this to improve the way I learn personally?

• How can I use this to improve the way I teach, train or communicate with other people?

   If people have such different learning styles, how can I best accommodate those preferences so that I reach the widest audience most effectively?

• What's the significance of this for children – whether my own, my future children or my immediate family?

> "A uniform way of teaching and testing is patently unsatisfactory when everyone is so different."
>
> **Dr Howard Gardner**
> *Frames of Mind*

NATURAL LEARNING

Write your name in the box below with your usual hand, ie: preferred hand.

*Now change the pen or pencil to the **other** hand and again, write your name.*

*What did you think and feel as you signed with your **non**-preferred hand? The task was probably rather awkward. It probably took longer and required more effort. The result was not as good.*

When people learn how to learn in their preferred style – the way that best suits their individual brain – it's like writing with your preferred hand. The result is much better, easier and quicker.

This book helps you to discover and use your preferred way of learning – to make it easier, more effective and, above all, more enjoyable. And how to do the same for others.

The Six Stages of Learning

From our analysis of the brain we have concluded that effective learning involves Six Stages. The Six Stages can be summarized by the acronym M.A.S.T.E.R. invented by Accelerated Learning Trainer Jayne Nicholl.

A Mind Set for Success

You need to be in a 'resourceful' state of mind. That state of mind is relaxed, confident and motivated. If you are stressed, or lack belief in your ability, or cannot see the point of what you are learning, you won't learn well.

Acquire the Facts

You need to take in the facts to suit your preferred learning style. There are differences in the extent to which we each need to see, hear, or get physically involved in what we are learning.

When you learn something new, you need to do something to make that information more memorable to yourself. What you will do depends on your preference for visual, auditory or physical learning – or whether a combination of all three works best for you.

Search out the Meaning

You need to explore what you are learning. There's a difference between knowing about something and truly understanding it.

When you thoroughly explore a subject, you turn surface knowledge into deep understanding. How you achieve this depends upon the unique way you use your range of intelligences.

Trigger the Memory

You now need to memorize the key elements of what you have learned. The aim is to commit one or two key facts to memory, so the rest of what you've learned comes flooding back.

Exhibit What you Know

You cannot be really sure you have really understood what you've learned unless you test yourself. You need to 'show you know'.

Reflect on <u>How</u> you Learned

Finally, you need to reflect on how well the learning went. The aim is to improve, not just what you know, but how you learn. That way you will become a better and better learner.

TOOLS EXTEND YOUR NATURAL POWER

A lever magnifies the power of your arms. A screwdriver increases the power of your hands. A torch amplifies the power of your eyes in the dark.

These tools of learning extend the natural power of the brain

In the remainder of the book you will find some powerful ideas which we know make learning easier. They make up a basic learning 'tool kit'.

They fit into a systematic approach to learning that involves six stages.

You can visualize the **M.A.S.T.E.R.** formula for effective learning as a loop. By reflecting on the way you can learn, you can make adjustments in order to get better at it each time.

A MIND SET for success

ACQUIRE the facts

REFLECT on how you learned

SEARCH out the meaning

EXHIBIT what you know

TRIGGER the memory

YOUR NOTES

"Active reading is a conversation with the author."
Consequently we invite you to use this page for notes and to ask yourself at least some of these questions.

What was the big idea? What was new?

What assumptions were made? Do I agree with them?

What was fact? Was the evidence reasonable? What was not clear?

What was opinion? Can I accept it? Was any issue oversimplified?

What are my main conclusions? What are the consequences?

How can I use what I've learned? For my personal learning? Training? At home?

What do I want to explore further?

Stage 1
A Mind Set for Success

Start with how you feel

How people feel about learning is extremely important. If you feel good about your ability to learn, this first section contains ideas that will reinforce and extend that confidence. But many others lack confidence as learners, so it's important that you know how to help them understand that they are not stuck with those feelings.

Henry Ford put it so well, "Whether you think you can, or whether you think you can't – you're probably right". People's mind set as they start to tackle any task is a key to their success.

A positive attitude to learning flows from:

1   Knowing how to create the strongest possible belief in your own ability. Self-belief is a key to success.

2   Being able to set clear goals. To spend time learning means choosing from competing possibilities. Your motivation to choose study over more immediate pleasures depends largely on how clear your vision of your future success is.

3   Being able to relax and calm yourself whenever you need.

NOTE

This book is not just meant to be read, but to be defaced! Write notes in it, argue with it and discuss it with your family and friends.

WORTH THINKING ABOUT!

- Walt Disney was fired by a newspaper editor because he lacked 'good creative ideas'.

- Einstein could not speak until he was four, and could not read until he was seven.

- Beethoven's music teacher told him he was "hopeless as a composer".

- Paul Gauguin only tried painting because he failed as a stockbroker.

- Rodgers and Hammerstein's first collaboration was so disastrous that they didn't work together again for years.

- Writer Marilyn Ferguson puts it well, "Your past is not your potential".

   High achievers are made – not born.

EVERYTHING IS POSSIBLE

Barbara Meister-Vitale was dismissed as a retarded child. She couldn't read at 12 and was pronounced as 'hopelessly dyslexic'.

Her grandmother never gave up on her – she encouraged her to use her talent to draw, create mental images, and to play music. Gradually she learned to use more of these visual and rhythmic talents to explore her school work. It helped reduce her reliance on the written word.

Today she is a member of MENSA, and has two degrees, including a Masters degree in early learning.

Feelings and self-belief

Try this:

Imagine you are in the kitchen. You take a fresh lemon from the fruit bowl. It is cool in your hand.

The yellow dimpled skin feels smooth and waxy. It comes to a small green conical point at either end.

The lemon is firm and quite heavy for its size as you look at it in the palm of your hand.

You raise the lemon to your nose. It gives off such a characteristic, unmistakeable citrus smell, doesn't it?

You take a sharp knife and cut the lemon in half. The two halves fall apart, the white pulpy outer skin contrasting with the drops of pale lemon coloured juice that gently ooze out.

You raise the lemon towards your mouth. The lemon smell is now slightly stronger.

Now you bite deeply into the lemon and let the juice swirl around your mouth. That sharp sour lemon flavour is unmistakeable.

Stop a minute.

The image of learning has tended to be of someone reading quietly, or sitting passively listening to a teacher.

That's not how it should be.

The biggest difference between good and poor learners is the extent to which they actively explore the subject.

Did your mouth water? Almost everyone's does. And yet the extraordinary thing is that if you were simply asked to 'make your mouth water', you couldn't have done it.

The 'imagery' worked because your emotional middle brain – an area where your beliefs are formed – does not distinguish between experiences that actually occur out there in the real world, and experiences you imagine vividly in your head.

You can use this fact to programme your emotional brain to believe very strongly in your success. You personally may not need to do it for learning – but it's a valuable skill in any area of your life.

Success comes in cans – not can'ts.

Because mathematics is such a common fear for many people, we have used it as an example.

If you are good at mathematics don't be smug – substitute a subject you feel you are not good at like public speaking or drawing.

(By the way, x = 5)

All attitudes are learned attitudes

If 2x – x = 5, what is x?

Many people feel tense in their stomach when they look at that equation. It can trigger a feeling of helplessness or even incompetence.

Yet these feelings towards mathematics (or public speaking) are merely unhelpful responses someone has learned from an original stimulus (occasion).

Similarly, when you hear people say, "I don't like public speaking", or "I don't like being in a training room – it reminds me of school", what they are really saying is "I don't like the **feeling** and **thoughts** I get when I'm faced with a speech or a training day".

The key point is this. The response you get from a stimulus isn't fixed. You learned it. And if you learned one response, you can learn another.

Just as people often **un**consciously generalize a single error into an overall feeling of defeat, so you can **consciously** generalize a single moment of success into a general feeling of confidence.

What success feels like

The picture in the margin is of someone at a moment of peak experience. A picture, in fact, of an athlete with tunnel vision. He can picture only one thing: Olympic Gold.

It's a state of exaltation, a state of 'flow', of knowing deep in your mind, deep in your body, that you have created a moment of excellence. It's a moment of great clarity, when everything came together in a moment of total **inner** satisfaction. That moment lives inside you forever.

That sort of moment is a powerful resource to draw upon. A memory that, if played over and over, will trigger the same feeling of powerfulness inside you. Because the memory of the moment and the feeling that goes with it are inseparable. The memory is the stimulus – the feeling is the response.

Replay the memory and you replay the feeling. Replay the feeling and you've created a resourceful state of mind. **A feeling of strength to draw on when you need.**

From the instant he left the starting blocks, Linford Christie knew he was going to win the 1992 men's 100 metre Olympic Gold Medal.

He had run and re-run the race in his mind over and over. His eyes were wide open with steely concentration on the finishing line. "All I had to do was focus", he said afterwards.

Any of the eight finalists could have won. But Christie had the mental edge. The vision.

 **ACTION**

Visualize a learning success

Before you go further, think back to a time when you did something that was exceptional. A time when everything 'clicked'. It all came together, and you surprised yourself with your own ability.

It could be a sporting moment. It could be a moment when you suddenly solved a problem, saw a solution in a flash of insight. Maybe you got an 'A' grade on a paper, or an exam result beyond your expectations.

It could be the exact moment in a negotiation when you suddenly knew you would succeed, a perfectly executed dance step – or the look on someone's face when they congratulated you on an achievement.

In other words, a peak moment. If you need help remembering, just look at the illustration above. That is the feeling. For a moment time stands still, and you have 'the force'.

I CAN'T
I CAN

You are not stuck with your feelings.

You can choose to change them!

Sometimes you can make important shifts in attitude through quite small changes.

You can change the word 'impossible' to 'I'm possible' with just one small apostrophe (').

Impossible I'm possible

Notice how you can change a negative to a positive with just a simple down stroke of the pen:

−   +

In a similar way, you can choose to change your feelings and attitudes. A positive state of mind will immediately make you more able to learn – or tackle anything new.

POSITIVE PROGRAMMING

You have used this 'technique' lots of times without realizing it. It is the same mental process that associates 'our song' with a particular evening, or a perfume with a particular event.

The song or the perfume always 'brings back' the same feeling. Now your 'cue' word and the successful image will bring back a confident feeling. You are merely consciously and deliberately using the same mental process for a positive reason.

ACTION

Now stop and re-create a vivid memory of your own learning success.

First re-create what you were **doing**.

Then re-create what you were **hearing**.

Then re-create what you were **seeing**.

Then re-create what you were **saying** to yourself.

Then re-create what your **body felt** like.

Finally, re-create the emotions you were **feeling**.

Creating a resourceful state of mind

You can create a confident, positive state of mind – whenever you choose – with this simple sequence.

Step 1   Recall your moment of success.

Step 2   Now intensify that memory. What did you **see** at that moment? What did you **hear**? What did you **feel**? Get as much detail as possible, using all your senses.

Avoid seeing yourself in the scene from a distance. It is **essential** that you look out at the successful scene with your own eyes – because that recreates the same feeling of competence and strength that you had originally.

You have learned how to recall a powerful state of resourcefulness. All you need now is a way to call that feeling up, whenever you wish.

Step 3   Having recaptured your moment and feeling of peak experience, think of **one** word that sums up the original event. That becomes your 'cue' word.

Step 4   Sit up straight and straighten your body. Pull your shoulders back. Now look up and take a deep breath. This is important, because at moments of peak experience, we automatically breathe deeply. (You probably already feel different!)

Step 5   Clench your fist – which is a natural thing to do when you feel powerful.

Step 6   Now intensify your memory of that original experience. Really **revel** in the powerful feeling. And say that cue word to yourself.

Step 7   Unclench your fist and open your eyes.

Repeat this sequence of seven steps, many times over the

next two days. The more often you repeat the sequence the stronger the stimulus/response pattern becomes.

Later, you will be able to return to this resourceful state whenever you wish. Just take a deep breath, picture the scene, clench your fist and say your cue word inside your head.

You've deliberately programmed yourself to feel confident and competent – on command. It's not just a skill for learning – it's a skill for life.

Positive affirmations

We all have an inner voice – the running commentary in our heads that accompanies our actions, like "Oh no, I'm going to mess this up" or "I feel good and I'm going to get this right".

This is good if what we're saying is positive, but much less helpful if we are negative about ourselves.

You can increase your chance of success in whatever you tackle by using **affirmations**. Affirmations are simply positive statements that express what you choose to become. An example is 'I am a confident public speaker.'

Repeating an affirmation for mental strength is like doing push-ups for physical strength.

You don't notice the difference immediately, but the results come with practice.

'I AM A CONFIDENT PUBLIC SPEAKER'

The affirmation need not be true for you yet – the time to use affirmations is when you are trying to achieve something.

At first, affirmations describe you as you would like to become. You say the affirmation to yourself (or out loud) over and over. The affirmation influences your thoughts and behaviour, and gradually becomes more and more true.

Top class athletes, sportsmen and sportswomen frequently use these techniques to help them towards success.

We have no problem in understanding how negative comments have a very real effect on people's thoughts and behaviour. If you tell someone that they are stupid or irresponsible, we all know they will come to be negative and act stupidly and irresponsibly. It's negative programming and it works all too well.

Positive affirmations merely use the same process, but **you** will be doing the programming to achieve a positive effect.

WHY AFFIRMATIONS WORK

Affirmations help create a more positive self-image. A self-image is the picture of yourself you hold in your subconscious (your limbic system or middle brain).

A good example of a simple, short, snappy, positive affirmation is, 'I am a confident learner'.

'I AM A CONFIDENT LEARNER'

The more you repeat your affirmation, the more comfortable you will feel with it. And the closer you will move towards achieving your ambition.

Repeat your affirmation to yourself whenever you are faced with a challenge.

At the beginning your conscious mind doesn't need to fully believe in them.

But with repetition your subconscious comes to accept your affirmations and looks for ways to make your actions match its beliefs.

So gradually a belief in yourself as, for example, a confident speaker, produces the actual result.

If your head has been full of one subject and you have to switch to learning another subject, a short period of calming and mind clearing is valuable.

Calm focus

You often feel tension where the head joins the body – in the neck and shoulders. That is especially true for students and people who work with computers.

If you clear away distracting tension, you are left with the ability to direct your energy more fully. And directed energy is simply a definition of concentration.

Since your physical well-being affects your brain work, here is a four-step sequence that will help you learn better by helping you create a state of **calm focus**.

1   Pay attention to that internal voice

The one that may be making negative, stress producing comments like – "Oh no, not a speech! I hate public speaking!" or "Oh no, not statistics, I'm useless at percentages".

Make sure you hear this type of 'subconscious sabotage'. Don't let your subconscious talk behind your back! You can't change what you're not aware of.

2   Physically shift your position

If you're sitting, stand. If you are standing, move. Your mind and body are so closely linked together, that by changing position you can often start to shift your thoughts towards new possibilities.

3   Maximize your oxygen

The brain only weighs three pounds, which is about 2% of your body weight. Yet it consumes 20% of your oxygen intake. So before each learning session (and throughout the day as needed), close your eyes and breathe deeply for just a minute or two.

Sit with your back well into the chair, spine straight. Let your jaw fall loose. Imagine there is a balloon in your stomach. As you breathe in, push your lower stomach out to its fullest limit. Then continue to take in air as your chest rises and expands. Keep breathing in until your chest is fully expanded, and your stomach is now sucked in.

Pause while you hold your stomach in for a moment. Then let the air out with a sigh. At the same time it might help to say the word '**calm**' slowly.

Continue this pattern for 5 - 10 breaths. After you have done this deep breathing, deliberately stiffen and straighten your back, and roll your eyes upwards towards the ceiling.

You will not only feel relaxed – you will feel strengthened and may well want to smile. The word 'inspired' comes from the Latin word meaning 'to breathe in'.

4   Replace any negative thoughts with your own affirmation

This four step sequence may take a maximum of one or two minutes. In that short time, however, you can create an important component of successful learning: a state of calm focus.

Establish your goal and write it down

You decided to learn something – but are you **really** clear why you are learning it? What's the benefit? What exactly is your aim? Better job prospects? More money? To make your work easier? To make it more enjoyable?

Think out your goal and write it down.

When you write down a goal you have to think it through more clearly. You can't be vague. The act of putting it on paper makes it more real, more concrete.

If it's a really important goal, put it on a postcard and stick it up where you will see it every day.

))» WII – FM «((

Someone once said, perceptively, that we all listen to Radio Channel WII - FM. It stands for 'What's In It – For Me?'.

Unless you have really thought through clearly the benefits of learning something, your motivation will be weak.

Create a vision

We all have a conscious and subconscious mind. Our conscious mind expresses itself in logical terms, eg: "I really should start learning French tonight" or "I need to study that engineering manual".

Our subconscious mind, however, is much more concerned about how we feel about ourselves. Are we comfortable, happy and safe? Or are we feeling unhappy, pressurized or threatened? Are we confident or apprehensive?

This is where the conflict takes place. To succeed you need to make sure that what you consciously **say** you want and what you **sub**consciously **feel** you want, are the same.

To succeed in a task it is important to create a motivating, vivid vision of your future. Such a vision helps programme your subconscious mind (the emotional limbic centre of your brain) to achieve the goals you have set for yourself.

GOAL SETTING IS FUNDAMENTAL

There is no point in being the most efficient oil rig team in history if you're drilling in the wrong place!

A ROUTE MAP FOR LIFE

What would you think of an airline pilot who took off without a destination and a basic route map?

Your life is a journey. It deserves some clear goals and specific written plans.

"You have to start with the end in mind."

Stephen Covey

Napoleon played out all his battles in his mind before they took place. He put it well, "Imagination is stronger than willpower".

So imagine your success, and you are already half way to achieving it.

Goals need to be written, seen and felt to be motivating.

"Establishing goals is all right so long as you don't let them deprive you of interesting detours!"

Doug Larson

To achieve what you want in life, you need to be committed. The willpower to succeed comes from a combination:

1   Have a **vision** of what you want to achieve.

2   Have a firm **belief** that you can achieve that vision.

People whom we describe as having terrific willpower simply have a clear vision of what they want, and believe they can do it. This is true of sticking to a fitness training schedule, a strict diet, studying at night school, or getting a qualification.

So now look at your written goals and visualize yourself as you'll be when you've succeeded. What will you look like, feel like?

If you have a vision, you have a purpose, and if you have a purpose, you create determination and willpower.

Create an action plan

You have a written goal and a motivating vision. Now you need an action plan to achieve those goals. An action plan is merely a set of steps you need to take to reach your specific, written, target(s).

To define the steps, you will need to ask yourself a simple question, "What prevents me from getting from where I am now, to where I want to be?"

Do I need:

*   Money – how much? Where do I get it?
*   Time – how do I free up time?
*   Knowledge – where from?
*   A skill – how do I acquire it?
*   Support – who among my family, friends, colleagues or supervisors can help?

An action plan should meet the **S.M.A.R.T** criteria, ie: it should be

Specific	What exactly will you do?
Measurable	How will you know when you've succeeded?
Achievable	Is it realistic?
Resourced	Have you allocated enough time and money?
	Have you got the information you need?
Timetabled	When will you have achieved each step?

Why all this planning is worth it!

When you have a goal, a vision, a written plan (with a weekly 'to do' list) your life has a greater sense of direction. Your goals, of course, will not stay fixed. You will change and modify them along the way, but any change will be **deliberate** and made by **you.**

What's more, when you have a goal, a vision and a plan it's much easier to distinguish between what's important, or merely urgent. Too often we break off from doing something that is important to deal with something that only **seems** urgent but is actually trivial. Like a telephone interruption.

Successful people know the difference between important and urgent! Important is when **you** allocate your own time. Urgent is when other people demand your time with stuff that could wait.

If your life is worth living, it's worth planning.

Here are three final thoughts to get the most out of your time.

1 **Use 'down time'**

   Fifteen minutes a day adds up to over 90 hours in the course of a year. In 15 minutes of waiting for a bus or a train, you could easily learn 10 words of a foreign language – if you wrote them out on flash cards. That's over 3,000 words learned in the course of a year. The basic vocabulary of an entire new language.

   What can **you** learn in your 'down time'?

2 **Set your own deadlines**

   Have you noticed how people manage to accomplish even large tasks when they are up against a deadline? They say proudly, "I did it in the end".

   They did – but they were being passive, not active. If they did it in the end, they could equally well have done it at the beginning! The person in control sets her own deadlines.

3 **Share your goals**

   When you discuss your goals with someone else, you automatically increase your motivation. It's now a 'public' commitment, and you do not want to let yourself down.

BEWARE OF WISHES!

What we say reveals more than we sometimes think. When someone says "I wish ..." what they usually mean is "I'd like to, but it's too much trouble".

When they say "I'll try ..." they usually mean "I'm warning you now I may fail". So when they do, they have a let-out clause ... "I only said I would try!"

THE TOP 2%

A recent study was published of the top 2% of 'achievers' – people who are acknowledged to be successful in their field.

Whilst they all had different successes, they all shared one thing in common. They all had written down their goals in life.

ALL LEARNING INVOLVES EMOTION

Researchers like Daniel Goleman and Paul MacLean have shown that your emotions need to be engaged to make learning stick in the memory.

That's why colour, art, music, enthusiasm, games, team work and fun – coupled with low stress – are so important in learning.

SUBCONSCIOUS PROMPTS

We pick up a lot of our knowledge from 'cues' that we are scarcely aware of. But they influence our state of mind all the same.

Try putting up a really beautiful poster or picture where you learn or study, or a memento of a past success.

Or some quotations that make you feel good.

There are lots of quotations scattered through this book.

We hope they are working!

Use any that you especially like to make your place of learning more attractive.

Catch yourself doing it right!

This simple but effective idea is adapted from *The One Minute Teacher* by Spencer Johnson. The idea is **deliberately** to look for occasions when you did something right or learned something well.

Having 'caught yourself doing it right', you simply praise yourself for it. Something straightforward will do like, "Helen, that was really good, well done".

The basis for this deceptively simple idea is very sound. If you want to change someone's behaviour, you do so by rewarding them when they get it right – not by punishing them when they get it wrong! Hence the value of noticing and praising each of your own (and other people's) successes.

Big changes rarely come in one leap. They are almost always made up of lots of small steps forward. The idea of 'catching yourself doing something right' recognizes this important truth.

The last word on state of mind!

Studies done by doctors Janice and Ronald Glaser at Ohio State Medical School prove how important it is to be able to control your state of mind. They showed that stress reduces the production of interferon, a chemical that's necessary for the efficient working of the immune system. Stress, therefore, weakens your body's resistance to disease.

In addition, the hormones most associated with anxiety (cortisol and adrenalin), have a depressing effect on the immune system. Small wonder then that colds and other more serious illnesses increase when people are stressed.

All this underlines the importance of the power you now have to create a resourceful and relaxed state of mind. **The power puts you in control**. And the feeling that you are in control of your life is a vital element in maintaining good health.

Dr George Vaillant showed in his book *Adaptation to Life* that mental health is the most important predictor of physical health.

Willpower =
Vision + Belief
in your own ability

TRAINING TIPS

Orchestrating the mind set

Look back on this section and ask yourself this question: "How can I make any training or teaching session I run more learner-friendly?"

Most trainers start with content. "**What** will I teach them?" The first question should be on the process: "**How** will I teach them? How can I create a mind set in my audience that's most conducive for learning?"

Here are a few ideas – but the best ideas will flow from your own conclusions from looking back on this first section.

You might:

- Send out some **information in advance** of the training so your learners have an idea of what to expect and some basic knowledge of the subject to build on in the training room.

  Maybe they could each create a learning map of what they already know? Could your 'advance communication' be an audio tape? Computer disc?

- **Ensure the room looks inviting** – flowers on the tables, music as they enter, posters on the wall with inspirational quotes. Seating not formal theatre style, but around tables for easy communication between trainees. You're not the focus, they are.

- Invite each trainee to state their **expectations and concerns** aloud. No one comes to a training session with a blank mind.

  They each have personal concerns ("Will this be worthwhile?") and expectations. If you put these expectations and concerns on a flip chart you can return to them at the end of the day and see how far you allayed their concerns and met their expectations.

  It's all part of an important principle. Make sure your learners have a feeling of control.

  Try this. Give your trainees a red card each. Then invite them quietly to raise their red card anytime they feel lost. That way they can signal they don't understand without drawing attention to themselves. And they feel in control.

  You also have an instant feedback on those areas where the group needs more instruction!

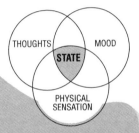

ALL LEARNING IS AFFECTED BY STATE OF MIND

Your audience's 'state' is the result of their thoughts, mood and physical comfort. You need to orchestrate all three to ensure they learn well.

Slouch down, droop your shoulders and think "This is boring!" How do you feel?

Now sit up, shoulders back, look up, smile and think, "This is fascinating". Now how do you feel? Your body and thoughts created two different states.

You can control other people's state – when you influence their thoughts, mood and physical posture.

When you talk everything 'speaks' to your audience – what you say and how you say it.

Since all learning is state-dependent, a good presenter will:

1 *Decide in advance what the audience will feel as well as know.*

2 *Build a rapport with the audience. You're the medium and therefore a key part of the message, so:*

- *Make frequent eye contact.*
- *Vary your tone and voice level.*
- *Use gestures to re-inforce the point.*
- *Lean forward and lower your voice to 'bring them into your confidence'.*
- *Use language – and actions – that involve visual, auditory and physical preferences, eg:*

  "Now picture this...
  "Here's a concrete point to grasp."
  "Listen, does this ring true to you?"

- *Include your audience with words like 'let's, we, us'.*
- *Be open, friendly, genuine.*

- **Explain the outcome** of the session on a poster in advance, ie: what they'll be able to do or what they'll know at the end. That's the vision.

- Ensure you fully **discuss the benefits** of the session so they have the motivation to pay attention. By no means are all trainees there voluntarily. Many are simply there because they were sent!

- Do the group have **sound learning strategies**? If the trainer and learners are both operating on the same framework for learning – ie: the M.A.S.T.E.R. model – they are in a position truly to collaborate. That's what really accelerates learning.

- **Vary the type of activity frequently** and **allow for a short break** every 20 minutes. This break can be reflective, eg: talking to a neighbour about the significance of what they have learned.

  Or it can be active, eg: participants can throw a soft ball to each other while they think up questions for others to answer, based on what they've learned. It's quick, energizing and yet productive.

- **Catch people 'doing it right'.** Have several fun, simple prizes to hand out when an individual or team shows they've learned a key point, or even collaborated well.

A training session that's low threat/high energy has a good learning atmosphere.

PARENT TIPS

Your child's mind set

Research shows that your child's attitude to learning and the degree to which you give her active support are one of the single biggest factors in her success: more important than family income, more important than the past academic achievement of the parents.

There are many ideas from this first section that you can use with your children – affirmations, calming strategies, helping them create a vision of themselves as successful learners of a subject, setting simple goals, using 'down time' and praising themselves for each step of achievement.

It is important to explain, simply, about learning styles and brain capacity. If a child thinks she can learn – she can. If a child has the appropriate learning strategies that match her learning style, then she will feel confident that she can influence and improve the way she learns.

And don't forget the importance of WII-FM. Discuss **why** each subject is worth learning.

Here is a story from our work in education that has important lessons. We took a poor performing class and let them spend some time discussing why the particular subject was worth learning. (**Motivation**)

Then we realised that our group simply didn't have a clear image of what 'A' grade work looked like or what to do to get it. So we invited some 'A' grade students of the same age group to explain what they did to get this grade. (**Vision**)

Next we told each of our class that they started with an 'A' in this subject. The only way they could lose it was to hand in sub-standard work. What's more, now they knew what 'A' grade work involved, they were to grade their own work before handing it in. (**Control**)

What a difference! Whereas they previously couldn't imagine ever getting a top grade they now actually had it. And, of course, they didn't want to let it go. From a position where the grade was handed down from above, they now felt they could personally influence the outcome of their work.

We went on to teach them how to grade and improve each other's work.

By giving them a clear vision of quality and the feeling that they controlled their own work, many of those previously failing students were re-motivated.

PRAISE EFFORT

It's important to celebrate not just end results, ie examination successes, but the process of learning and trying.

Praise should not be vague but should contain specific guidance and should reinforce what your child did well, eg: "Well done, you got that right because you read the question properly before you started".

So look for occasions to praise effort.

Watch a professional football game. Celebrating moments of success is a major element in building a team spirit.

If it's worth learning – it's worth celebrating.

M.A.S.T.E.R.
Mind Set

YOUR NOTES

"Active reading is a conversation with the author."
Consequently we invite you to use this page for notes and to ask yourself at least some of these questions.

What was the big idea? What was new?

What assumptions were made? Do I agree with them?

What was fact? Was the evidence reasonable? What was not clear?

What was opinion? Can I accept it? Was any issue oversimplified?

What are my main conclusions? What are the consequences?

How can I use what I've learned?   For my personal learning?   Training?   At home?

What do I want to explore further?

Stage 2
Acquire the Facts

What's the core idea – the big picture?

Like most books this book has a contents page, sub-headings, illustrations and diagrams.

They are all useful when you are trying to build up an initial impression of the subject and establish the core idea.

The core idea is vital because once you've understood it everything else falls into place and 'makes sense'. The core idea of this book is on page 2 in the introduction in a box.

So start with a short scan-read of any new book to determine its core idea.

If you are learning from a training session or a demonstration, you can get an overview from the trainer or teacher.

Ask for a general outline before the instructor launches into the session. A useful question to ask is "What do you want me to know or be able to do after the session?" What are her objectives for you? What's the core idea?

Scan-read a book or chapter first. It gives you the feel of the subject.

You are looking for clues.

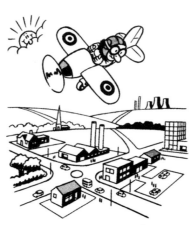

Get the big picture first

Sketch out what you already know

Jotting down what you already know gives you a clearer picture of your start point. It builds confidence, and it helps define what you don't know!

Spend a minute jotting down what you already know about *learning styles, learning and training.* What don't you know? What needs more of your attention?

If you have 'scan-read' ahead, you will be able to do this.

BUT DON'T JUMP TO CONCLUSIONS!

Getting an overall picture – or feel – of the subject is important. But remember, you haven't got the detail yet.

So don't jump to firm conclusions until you have explored the subject properly.

Many people's main form of exercise is jumping to conclusions!

You have only seen the wood – now you need to examine the trees!

If you are learning from a lecture or a training session you should make your notes in the five minutes before it starts. A preliminary learning map (see page 41) of the subject would be a good way to sketch what you already know. Then, as you explore the subject in more depth, you can keep adding to your learning map. The map grows as your knowledge grows.

Break it down into small steps

The Chinese philosopher Lao Tzu once said, "A journey of a thousand miles starts with a single step". However daunting a task may appear, you can crack it with a simple step-by-step plan.

One researcher has calculated that a child of six has learned more facts about her world than the number of facts needed to acquire a medical degree! It's probably true. She did it, and you did it, bit by bit. Start with the basics and work up.

The important point is that when you are learning something challenging – you **don't** automatically have to start at the beginning. Roam around the subject and get started on something that engages your interest.

Keep interested – ask questions!

How do you stay concentrated? Indeed, how do you get interested in a subject you 'have' to learn?

The easiest way to stay focused is continuously to develop questions.

The trick is to write down these questions on a separate piece of paper. They act as a motivator – keeping your brain focused on the trainer, teacher or text book, looking for the answers.

If a child just glances at the sky, she might fleetingly notice that it is cloudy. If she really **looks** at the sky, she'll notice how the clouds change shape, and wonder why the shapes can change so dramatically. That can lead to an interest into how wind and temperature combine to form the various cumulus, stratus or nimbus clouds we see.

Why does the weather mainly come from the West in the Northern hemisphere? Is the direction of weather reversed in the southern hemisphere? What makes a sunset so beautiful? Why is it made up of reds and oranges?

If you only glance at a garden, you might notice it is 'rather nice'. If you really look at a garden, you will see the incredible symmetry of a flower, the geometry of a spider's web in the morning dew, and maybe wonder whether there is a mathematical order to nature.

Why? What? How? Suppose?

"Constant questioning is the first key of wisdom."

Abelard

SMALL STEPS

Progress is rarely doing one thing 100% better. It's doing 20 things 5% better each.

Einstein was not a particularly hot scholar at school. But something sparked his interest in physics. It was a favourite toy – a magnet. He became interested in what forces caused the magnet to attract metal. So he started to think and wonder.

Einstein's brain now lies in a glass jar in a University in Mid America. It's no bigger than average, but researchers say that it shows evidence of very rich connections between the brain cells.

Other geniuses had favourite toys or games.

The inventor of the telephone, Alexander Graham Bell, had an uncle who would pretend to make his dog speak by manipulating its larynx.

Many years later he remembered this when he was thinking of how to create the telephone.

Interrogate the subject

You see the point. A surface glance, and you can stay bored with a subject. But the harder you look, the more interested you become. Sometimes you have initially to force yourself to get into the detail – but once you start really looking, you get 'hooked'. You start to wonder and explore, and that's learning.

Imagine you are an interviewer. Your job is to make sure the author or lecturer does not get away with vague statements or half truths. So keep asking questions like:

- "How do we know this is true?"

- "If it's true, what else follows?"

- "Is that conclusion justified?"

- "What assumptions are being made?"

- "What additional arguments could I think of?"

- "Is this fact or opinion?"

- "How could I use this?"

- "Is this logical?"

- "Do I agree with this?"

- "How much evidence is there for what is being said?"

- "Can I think of any (better) examples to illustrate the argument?"

When you read to answer a question or solve a problem you read with a sense of purpose, ie: with **interest**.

It is easy to make up questions. Simply take the main heading of the section and turn it into a question. For example, a question to ask about this section is, "**Why** should I ask questions?" or "**How** will it help me learn?" or even "**How** do I make up questions?"

When you listen to a teacher or trainer with questions in front of you, you automatically concentrate better.

Probably the biggest difference between 'natural' or 'informal' learning, and 'formal' or 'academic' learning is this: in natural learning situations you are almost always able to ask questions, and often there is someone else available to explain it to you.

"I'd rather know some of the questions than all of the answers."

George Bernard Shaw

STAY ACTIVE

Effective reading is a conversation with the author.

WHAT DO YOU PREDICT?

A good way to stay focused on the subject is to stop every now and then and predict what the author, trainer or teacher is going to say.

Multi-sensory learning

Assigned text books can be boring. If you are turned off by a subject you need to master, seek out a different, lighter, clearer book on the subject.

If you're learning something new, by definition, it involves taking in information from the outside. So you're either reading, listening, watching or doing. You're using your senses.

Consequently, one aspect of a personal learning style is your preference for visual, auditory or physical learning (also called kinesthetic learning). Other people will have different preferences.

The ideal, normally, is to focus all your senses on the learning task.

Here's a summary of what researcher Dr Vernon Magnesen of the University of Texas found out about memory. Although remembering something is not the same as learning something, the implications are clear.

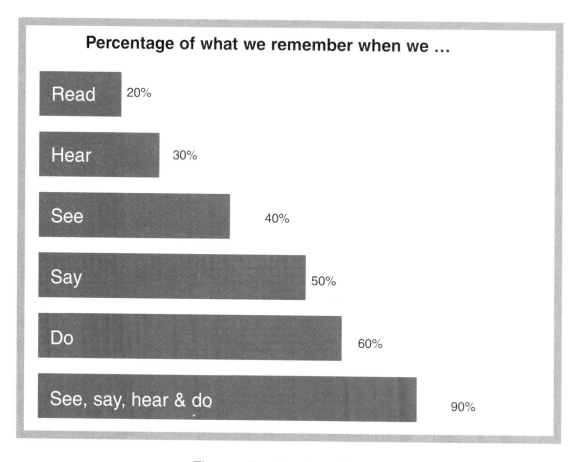

Percentage of what we remember when we ...

Read	20%
Hear	30%
See	40%
Say	50%
Do	60%
See, say, hear & do	90%

The question, therefore, is how can you learn in a way that combines: seeing, hearing, saying and doing?

Look at the next page and use multi-sensory learning to learn to count from one to 10 in Japanese in just two minutes!

Counting in Japanese

If the following information were presented as we've done in columns 1 and 2 below it would look very daunting and strange. As we've seen, when you're under threat your brain doesn't work to anywhere near full capacity.

Instead, now involve all your senses. Go to columns 4 and 5. Say the words as you mime the action. Start by saying "Itchy knee" as you scratch your knee (that's 1 and 2 in Japanese).

Then say "Sun, she go rock" as you point to the sun, point to or think of a woman, walk two steps and then shake your hips in a Rock and Roll action (that's 3, 4, 5 and 6). Now do a double 'sneeze', that's 7.

Now mime the action of putting on a hat for 8 (hatchi). Next coo like a dove (9). Finally, visualize or mime putting on a Jewish cap – Ju (10).

Repeat this exercise twice more while looking at the words. Then turn away from the page, and repeat the words and actions twice.

Counting from 1-10 in Japanese

(1) Japanese	(2) Japanese (sound)	(3) English	(4) You say:	(5) Action
一 壱	ichi	one	itchy	Scratch your
二 弐	ni	two	knee	knee
三 参	san	three	sun	Point to sky
四	shi	four	she	Point to woman
五	go	five	go	Walk two paces
六	roco	six	rock	"Rock 'n' Roll"
七	shichi	seven	shi-chi	Double sneeze
八	hachi	eight	hat-chi	Put on hat
九	kyu	nine	coo	Coo like a dove
十 拾	ju	ten	ju	Imagine a Jewish cap

The whole exercise should take about two to three minutes! And you've learned the basics of counting in Japanese, because 11 is ju-ichi, 12 is ju-ni. You did it so quickly because you involved **all** your senses.

Which are your preferred senses?

For each question on this and the next page, there are three answers. Circle or tick the answer that most closely represents you. When you have finished, total up the number of responses in each column – visual, auditory or physical.

The sense you chose most is likely to be your preferred or dominant learning sense – the sense you are normally most comfortable using to take in information.

Preferred senses test			
When you...		**Do you...**	
	Visual	**Auditory**	**Physical**
Spell a word	Try to visualize it (does it 'look' right).	Sound it out (does it 'sound' right).	Write it down (does it 'feel' right).
Are concentrating	Get most distracted by what's around you.	Get most distracted by noises.	Get most distracted by movement, or physical disturbance.
Choose a favourite art form	Prefer paintings.	Prefer music.	Prefer dance/sculpture.
Reward someone	Tend to write praise on their work in a note.	Tend to give them oral praise.	Tend to give them a pat on the back.
Talk	Talk quite fast, but keep idle conversation limited. Use lots of images, eg: it's like a needle in a haystack.	Talk fluently with an even pace, in a logical order and with few hesitations. Enunciate clearly.	Use lots of hand movements, talk about actions and feelings. Speak more slowly with longer pauses.
Meet people	Remember mostly how they looked/ the surroundings.	Remember mostly what was said/ remember their names.	Remember mostly what you did with them/remember their emotions.
See a movie, watch TV or read a novel	Remember best what the scenes/what people looked like.	Remember best what was said – and how the music sounded.	Remember best what happened/the characters' emotions.
Try to interpret someone's mood	Mainly note their facial expression.	Listen to their tone of voice.	Watch body movements.
Are recalling something	Remember what you saw/people's faces/how things looked.	Remember what was said/ people's names/jokes.	Remember what was done, what it felt like.
Are memorizing something	Prefer to memorize by writing something repeatedly.	Prefer to memorize by repeating words aloud.	Prefer to memorize by doing something repeatedly.

Preferred senses test

When you...	Do you...		
	Visual	**Auditory**	**Physical**
Are angry	Become silent and seethe.	Express it in an outburst.	Storm about, clench your fists, throw things.
Are inactive	Look around, doodle, watch something.	Talk to yourself or others.	Fidget, walk about.
Express yourself	Often use phrases like: *I see/ I get the picture/ Let's shed some light on this/ I can picture it.*	Often use phrases like: *That sounds right/ I hear you/ That rings a bell/ Something tells me/ It suddenly clicked.*	Often use phrases like: *That feels right/ I'm groping for an answer/I've got a grip on it/I need a concrete example.*
Are learning	Prefer to read, to see the words, illustrations, diagrams, sketch it out.	Like to be told, attend lectures, talk it over.	Like to get involved, hands on, try it out, write notes.
Assemble new equipment	First look at the diagrams/read the instructions.	First ask someone to tell you what to do. Then talk to yourself as you assemble it.	First work with the pieces.
TOTAL RESPONSES			

Visual learners like drawing diagrams, pictures and charts and watching films.

Visual/Verbal learners like to read the written word. They like books, posters with slogans, instruction material with clearly written text.

Auditory learners like to hear new information through spoken explanations, commentaries and tapes. They benefit from reading key passages aloud and making tapes.

Physical learners like hands-on learning where they can immediately try things for themselves.

They like to do as they learn, eg: writing, underlining, doodling, imagining.

The above test is only indicative. You should use it in conjunction with a careful observation of what works best for you. Try out the ideas in this book and note the ones that make learning more effective and easier for you. That's the real test.

Multi-sensory learning can be as simple as:

- Read and visualize the material ...   you have **seen** it.
- Read key points out loud, make up questions and answer them ...   you have **heard** it.
- Write out the main points on cards and arrange them in a logical order ...   you have **done** it.

"I learned not from those who taught, but from those who talked with me."

St Augustine

KEEP LOOKING BACK ...

Every now and then stop and take a short break.

Before you start again briefly review what you have just learned. You revise the subject – and get a motivating sense of progress.

... And forward!

If you also flick forward briefly you are setting your brain up for the subject.

It's the equivalent of a warm-up to a runner.

Getting the facts through your preferred senses

When you first encounter a book, a lecture or a training demonstration, you need to do something **extra** that helps you learn in a way that suits you best. Otherwise you will be merely passively reading or listening – and that's not learning!

Although some people have very strong learning preferences, 'multi-sensory' learning normally provides the best chance for successful learning. Multi-sensory learners deliberately engage all their senses as they learn. They V.A.P. it.

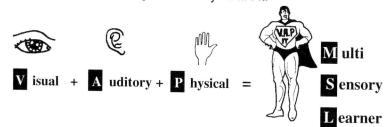

V isual + **A** uditory + **P** hysical = **M** ulti **S** ensory **L** earner

Here are some ideas to try. They are extra learning strategies for you to choose, depending on your personal preferences.

Tick it off!

If you have a text book or large instruction manual to tackle, make a light pencil tick at the end of each paragraph that you have fully understood. It is a signal to your brain to lock that information away. What's more, you can identify exactly where it was you started to get lost. Just after the last tick!

Instead of feeling overwhelmed by a whole chapter you can concentrate on understanding small chunks at a time.

Use a highlighter pen

If the book is your own, using a highlighter can be helpful. When you look back on the material a day, a month, or even a year later – you will have highlighted the important bits of **new** important information.

Notice the emphasis on the word new. Many people highlight all the important ideas in a paragraph. That sounds logical, but it isn't. The point about learning is that you are acquiring new information or new ways of looking at old information.

HIGHLIGHTS

Do not highlight or underline the first time you scan read a paragraph or section. Do it when you read for the ideas.

The advantage of highlighting is that when you come to want to review your notes later you only need glance at the highlighted ideas.

Result? You can revise your knowledge of a whole book in 15 minutes or so.

So to highlight something you already know is only going to increase your work load when you come back for a quick review later. And a quick review of what you've been learning is an essential part of really 'locking it all down'.

Highlighter pens also add colour, which appeals to the emotional part of your brain.

Read it dramatically

We remember what's dramatic. A pastel floral dress may be pretty, but it probably isn't memorable. A single crimson flower on a black dress would be memorable.

Just as visual images can be memorable, so can sounds. So if a passage is crucial or difficult – try reading it out dramatically. You can even use a foreign accent or whisper it. (We often whisper what's important!) Because a whisper or a foreign accent would be unusual, you'll remember it.

Summarize it out loud

Do you remember the statistics on sensory learning? We tend to remember more than twice as much of what we say aloud than of what we merely read.

So stop regularly and summarize out loud what you have read.

Walk about while you read or listen

Learners with a preference for physical learning need some way to express that preference.

Try walking about. Certainly get up and move every 25 – 30 minutes.

If it's appropriate to the subject, draw a chart or graph or even stop and mock up a simple model. Experiment with how much **you** need a physical element as you take in information. For example, a desk or table may not work as well for you as a lap board.

Make notes on 'post its' or postcards

'Post its' are little yellow sheets of paper made up into pads. Because these yellow 'post its' are small, they force you to reduce your notes to a very brief form. The key words jump out at you when you look back at them.

If you stick them all on a large sheet of paper they allow you to sort out your thoughts physically.

Writing key ideas on post cards and then sorting them out on a table works equally well. And you can stick the cards or post it notes on the wall where you learn as reminders.

A FOG SIGN!

Every now and again everyone gets lost. You just can't figure out what the text means. Develop your own sign for this.

A question mark or exclamation mark perhaps. Put it in the margin then come back later.

AUDIO AID

Tape recorders are great for auditory learners.

Tape your summary notes and play them back in the car.

DON'T IGNORE BOREDOM

Our brains don't work flat out all the time.

If you find you are getting bored, stop, get up, and take a break.

Then ask yourself which aspect of the subject is interesting. What is relevant? And switch for a time to that.

Sit quietly and visualize

Most of us need to sit and think quietly over what we have just seen, read or heard. Go over it in your mind's eye and make a 'mental movie' of it. It's a bit like an instant replay in a sports programme. It helps to store the information in your visual memory.

MENTAL IMAGERY

Flight crew achieve 100% pass rate!

Airline flight attendants need to know the location of over 60 pieces of emergency equipment.

Flight attendants boosted their pass rate from 70% to 100% by adding Step 4 to the following sequence.

1 They toured the plane noting the safety locations.
2 They filled in the location diagrams from memory.
3 They checked them against the master diagram.
4 They then sat, closed their eyes and visualized the original tour in their mind's eye. Finally, they filled in the location diagram again.

How can **you** add mental imagery the next time you learn something?

The learning maps in this book are professionally produced. They work just as well when you make them yourself with just words.

Learn with a friend

You will expand the range of questions you develop by discussing them with a friend. Your discussion will probably prompt further questions that neither of you would have thought of alone.

We remember up to 90% of what we see, say, hear and do. So tackle learning with a friend and dramatically increase your chance of remembering what you learn.

Learning maps

The essential rule in making a learning map is **only** to use **key words**. Key words are the essential words which – when you read them – remind you of the whole idea. The words that get to the heart of the meaning.

WHAT'S IMPORTANT?

The secret is to read ideas – not words.

Key words are usually nouns, and since nouns are names of things, they are easier to remember. The aim in effective note-taking is to strip away all the unnecessary words. It's like digging for gold. You get rid of all the surrounding earth to expose the nuggets of valuable information.

Most people take notes that contain **far** too many words. That is a mistake because:

*   You waste too much time writing it out in the first place.

*   If you write too much you will be concentrating more on the words than on the meaning of what the author, teacher or trainer is saying.

You don't need many words to remember – as long as they are ... THE KEY WORDS. They unlock a lot of memory.

*   You waste too much time re-reading the notes later.

How to make your own learning map

1   Draw a picture, symbol and/or write a phrase in the centre of the paper to stand for the topic.

2   Strip away everything except the key words. This is the most important rule.

3   Take the main ideas associated with the topic and let them branch out from the central idea. Express things with a picture, a symbol or key word or phrase on your map. Use only one or two key words per idea. This is the second most important rule.

4   Stop and think. Add new thoughts like branches on a tree. Put questions on areas you don't understand properly.

5   Organize your map – you may want to group some ideas that seem to go together, draw lines and/or arrows to represent connections between thoughts.

6   Usually you will now want to redraw your learning map. Don't resent this – it is a good way to help it stick in your long-term memory.

7   Use as much colour and as many symbols and pictures as possible. Our brains find these memorable. Aim to make each page of these notes look different.

8   Use bold and capital letters.

9   Don't crowd the page – leave space.

10 Use the paper horizontally – it gives you more space. And use one side of the paper – so you can use your learning maps as posters – or spread out a number of them in sequence.

TRY IT!

It is essential to experiment with learning maps.

The first time you try anything it feels strange and may take a little longer.

That's true of riding a bike or driving. First it seems odd – gradually it becomes familiar and natural.

So persevere – it's worth it.

ACTION

First pick a topic you are familiar with, such as yourself – your life, family, interests, job, etc. Then experiment by making a learning map about it.

A learning map is a tool to turn ideas and facts into an easily remembered VISUAL pattern of words.

You can jump about from one idea cluster to another and literally 'see' the connection between one idea and another.

It is also a tool to allow you to create a logical order for those ideas. Powerful stuff!

LOTS OF USES

Learning maps can also be very useful to plan speeches, presentations, agendas, reports or papers.

TAKING OR MAKING NOTES?

There is an important difference between taking notes and making notes.

Taking notes implies copying down other people's thoughts and opinions.

Making notes is when you turn their information into your own thoughts and opinions.

The main advantages of learning maps

The information is all on **one** page. The theme, the core idea, is at the centre, and the ideas that follow from that main theme are clustered around it.

Because the information is visual, it's possible to take it in all at once, and after a little study, to picture it in your mind's eye. This is especially easy when you have constructed the learning map yourself.

Because you get used to reading or listening for only the essential **ideas,** you learn to cut out irrelevant material. That's great for concise reports and getting to the **meaning** of the subject. You can also add new words (ideas) anywhere, at any time.

You begin to impose **your** order on other people's messy thoughts! The shape of the argument will literally begin to emerge. The definition of 'meaningful' is something that fits into a pattern or order that **you** create. You turn someone else's ideas into your own.

If you need to rework your original draft learning map, the very act of finding more logical ways of grouping the ideas together helps you figure out their meaning. And because they now become your ideas, they are easier to remember. You can actually summarize a whole book on a one page learning map. That makes them great for revising.

Know when to stop!

There are times in every learning situation when you simply can't make head or tail of it.

The right approach is not to struggle grimly with it for hours and end up with a bad case of depression, but to move on and come back later. The next section of the book may be much easier to understand. More importantly, it may contain clues that help you understand the bit you got stuck on.

You rarely have only one chance to understand something. So write down what you **don't** understand, and come back to it in a day or so. Or write it down and ask a friend or expert for help.

... but do come back later!

Researcher E M Gray searched for years for the one **single** factor that all successful people shared. Here it is.

Successful people simply do the things that less successful people don't like and can't be bothered to do. Successful people don't necessarily like doing them either! But their vision of success is stronger than their inertia. **They stick at it.**

A little girl visited a farm with her father. Out of a clutch of a dozen eggs, all had hatched but one.

"I'll help it, Daddy," said the little girl and gently cracked the egg open. In the night the duckling died. The struggle to be born is a vital part of the process of creation. It simply doesn't work without effort.

Nothing worthwhile gets created without persistence. Nothing worthwhile is learned in 'five easy lessons'!

The very word 'worth*while*' means that the subject is 'worth a *while*'.

DEALING WITH DISTRACTING THOUGHTS

If thoughts keep intruding on your learning, don't ignore them.

Acknowledge the thought, get up, move about and breathe deeply. Then let the thought go as if it were a balloon floating upwards.

"Luck favours the backbone, not the wishbone!"

"The only place where success comes before work is in the dictionary!"

Vidal Sassoon

"The fruit of the tree is out on a limb! All learning and change involves risk."

TRAINING TIPS

Transmitting the facts

Again, look back at the strategies for effective learning. What training strategies will match them? Do you, for example, have the core idea on a poster?

Some ideas of our own:

- Provide a wall chart with a 'big picture' overview. Global learners need it. What's the sequence of what they'll learn? One trainer created a frieze along the wall at the front of the training room previewing the most important topics.

- Have two groups compete to create a learning map of what they already know about the subject.

    Some trainers find this threatening. "What if the trainees already know most of what I'm going to say?"

    If they do, they'll only be bored – so it's better to know what they don't know so you can better tailor the day to what the groups actually need. That's part of the learner feeling in control.

- Create three checklists. Head them up:

VISUAL?   AUDITORY?   PHYSICAL?

How are you going to ensure all three sensory preferences are met?

Visual – Have you enough diagrams, charts, posters and overheads? Have you built in any imagery sessions? (see page 68)

Auditory – There's usually more than enough lecture in most training sessions! Have you built in anecdotes and stories? Do you invite your trainees to summarize each main section out loud? Do you continuously vary your tone and pace?

Physical – Have you planned frequent short sessions where trainees compare conclusions, or notes?

'Jigsaw' is an excellent physical (and interpersonal) activity. You pair up the learners. Half of a text is given to one learner, half to another. They learn their own parts and teach each other.

A successful follow-up to this is where a whole group of such pairs comes together and plays 'Challenge Match'. In this game the group is split into two teams who compete to think up

One trainer makes up cards with key facts on them and hangs them from the ceiling on a fishing line!

His trainees are surrounded by relevant information.

GAMES MOTIVATE

Whenever you incorporate a game into a learning session you increase motivation.

20 questions of fact to stump the opposition. It's a wonderful way to turn a dry training manual into a treasure chest of facts for a game.

Have you developed 'partial' hand-outs or learning maps? These are hand-outs and notes with gaps in them so the learners have to listen attentively and fill in the missing information.

Reflection time – It's important for trainers to allow for regular periods of reflection where learners have time to think through what they've learned and consolidate it.

Most speakers or trainers have experienced occasions where their audience appear inattentive. They fidget or look away. Often the trainer's reaction is to speed up or speak louder.

Their audience probably needs the opposite. They are being overloaded and their apparent inattention is because they need a quiet period properly to digest the information.

PARENT TIPS

Acquiring the facts

Again there are many ideas here that will really help your child.

Does she understand the core idea of the subject? Does she keep asking questions as she learns? Does she realize that she doesn't have to wait to be taught? That her teacher is only one source of information, and the library, CD-ROMs and the Internet are equally valid ways to learn?

What are his sensory preferences? Which learning strategies work best? Get him to experiment with a wide range, because different tasks call for different strategies.

Play games that encourage visualization. For example, 'Mental Hide and Seek' is a good game for young ones on a car journey. You simply think of somewhere you have hidden a small object in your house. His job is to guess where.

A simple game like this actually helps improve a child's spelling – because good spellers are adept at making a visual image of the word in their heads.

VISUALS

"Don't picture a white elephant with red stripes."

You can't **not** do it!

An estimated 90% of the information reaching our brain is from visual sources.

So a lecture without visual back-up is unlikely to engage people's attention for long.

MULTI-SENSORY LEARNING WORKS

A school in the UK Midlands area set up a one year comparison test between Accelerated Learning's German Language course versus conventional materials.

68% of the Accelerated Learning students achieved the top grades (and all passed).

Only 11% of students using conventional materials got top grades.

In a further study students using Accelerated Learning's Italian course all passed after just two terms of study – 63% at A grade. The course usually takes three years!

Teach her how to make a learning map, how to draw diagrams and how to make notes on post cards. Make up audio tapes for the car and teach her to summarize things out loud.

Above all encourage your child to become conscious of what ideas and techniques seem to work best for her.

SUPER SKILL 1

Power reading

Can you develop the capacity to speed read? Is it worthwhile?

The first question is easy to answer. Yes, you can easily triple or quadruple your reading speed. The answer to the second question is – "It depends".

Speed reading is a very useful skill for scan reading and it normally also prevents boredom. Since the brain thinks faster than the average person reads, there is too much temptation for the mind to wander. Keep it occupied by reading fast and concentration is automatically improved.

However, speed reading would not be desirable if you wanted to hear the words in your head. And such a strategy is often helpful or necessary for difficult mathematical or scientific texts. **Different speeds suit different purposes.**

Why we read slower than we need

The eye takes in information much faster than the ear. Yet many of us still want to 'hear' the words in our mind as we read them, even when we don't need to. We may not literally sub-vocalize or murmur the words under our breath – but it produces the same result.

By insisting on 'hearing' each individual word, we significantly slow down our reading. We can only 'hear' words at approximately 250 words to the minute, but we can see them at the rate of 2,000 words a minute or more. If you learn to read on a purely visual basis you can rapidly increase your reading speed.

Another problem is that we usually insist on trying to 'see' every word on a line. Yet you do not have to see every word to make sense of what you are reading. The mistake is to read words. It's not normally the individual words that matter, it is the **ideas** that those words convey.

Woody Allen once said he had taken a speed reading course and had read 'War and Peace' in 20 minutes.

"What's it about?"

"Russia," replied Woody.

COMPREHENSION

Speed reading is not the aim. The aim is speed comprehension.

If you only read the key words, you would cut the number of words you needed to read by at least 70% – and thereby triple or quadruple your reading speed. You read, not to see every word, but to **understand** the sense of the material. Remember in constructing learning maps, the key words are a small proportion of the whole.

A third problem is that the eye does not take in a line of print in a smooth flowing movement. In fact only the information reaching a specific and small area of the retina (called the fovea) is seen really sharply. The eye must stop for a fraction of a second to focus a small amount of text on the fovea.

Therefore, your eye movement is actually made up of a series of skips thus:

The dots are where the eye actually stops to register a strong image in the fovea. The words around these points of fixation are what is called your 'field of peripheral vision'.

Because we read in a series of skips or jerks, we are often tempted to back-skip, to check whether we really saw or understood some of the previous words. This back-skipping is common and probably cuts our reading speed down by a third.

There are a lot of redundant words in any text. These are words that merely join up ideas but don't contribute anything new.

How to speed read

You can measurably increase your reading speed in the next 20 minutes by carrying out the two following simple instructions. Choose a book you want, or need, to read. This one will do fine.

Start reading each line of print, not at the very beginning of the line, but two or three words in from the beginning. Your peripheral vision, and the redundant words, will ensure you miss no meaning.

Similarly finish reading two or three words from the end of the line. You will, therefore, have reduced the amount of text you need to fixate on, and hence increase your reading speed, without sacrificing any comprehension.

Add a physical aid by putting your hand flat on the page and move it forwards and backwards across the page in a sweeping motion, as illustrated. Move your hand down the page at a steady speed.

Start to run your hand down the page at an ever increasing speed. It must be much faster than you feel it is possible to register anything.

Allow your eyes to follow the tips of your fingers down the page, but keep within the limits of your 'sweeping' motion. Increase the speed until you are spending only four or five seconds per page!

Continue this simple speed training for 20 minutes. This is an absolutely essential part of the training.

If you try it for just two or three minutes, you cannot achieve the effect you are looking for.

At this rate you will initially perceive everything as a blur. Yet if you persevere you will find a strange thing happening.

A few words will begin to stand out on each page and they will be some of the key words. It is interesting proof that your brain is actually processing much of the printed page.

This high speed training succeeds in three ways. First it prevents any possibility of back-skipping. Secondly, it starts to break the dependence on 'hearing' the words in your head. You are now relying purely on visual reading, which is essential to achieve a really fast reading speed.

The third effect is comparable to the effect of driving down the motorway at a continuous high speed. When you do come to slow down to a 'normal' speed, you find that what you thought was 30 miles per hour, is in fact 60 miles per hour, or more. You have altered your perception of speed.

In the same way, when you go back to reading at your 'normal speed' – after twenty minutes of very high speed reading – you will find that it is measurably faster than your previous speed.

Power reading

Power reading is speed comprehension. It is invaluable for today's educational or business environment where an increasing amount of reading matter creates great pressure to 'keep-up-to-date'.

Power reading is an eight-step process. Let's see how it would work for an important 250 page textbook, made up of 10 chapters of 25 pages each.

1   **Create the big picture** of the book you are reading, ie: get the overview. **What's the core idea?**
    Approx time taken: 5-10 mins

2   **Preview** the material. Scan read the text of the first chapter at the rate of about six seconds a page. You are looking for key facts and ideas. You are looking to see whether this book will **add** to your knowledge. Maybe it won't, in which case you can abandon it early without wasting time!
    Approx time taken per chapter: 3 mins
    Time taken for the book: 30 mins

3   **Sketch** out what you know.
    Approx time taken per chapter: 3 mins
    Time taken for the book: 30 mins

4   **Set up your questions.** eg: What are the main ideas? What supporting evidence is there? Are the facts up-to-date? Are the conclusions justified? What's new? What can I use from this?
    Approx time taken per chapter: 3 mins
    Time taken for the book: 30 mins

BREAK THE SPEED LIMIT!

Florence Schale from Northwest University in America has studied readers extensively.

In *The Psychology of Reading Behaviour* she reported that most people were capable of reading at 1800 - 2000 words a minute.

That's eight times the normal speed under the restriction of 'auditory' reading, ie: reading and trying to hear the sound of words in your head.

*Being **selective** in what you need may be the best route to speed reading.*

5   **Read** the text of each chapter, one chapter at a time. Go at a pace of about 15 - 20 seconds a page. At this stage you can underline new ideas and put in ticks or question marks.
Approx time taken per chapter: 8 minutes
Time taken for the book: 80 mins

6   **Afterview.** Read back over the chapter, stopping at difficult sections and understanding the way the ideas and arguments connect, ie: establish the **pattern** to the argument. Read aloud parts that were difficult to understand.
Approx time taken per chapter: 8 mins
Total time taken for the book: 80 mins

7   **Make your notes.** In learning map form if that suits you.
Approx time taken per chapter: 10 mins
Total time taken for the book: 100 mins

8   **Review.** Spend 10 minutes the next day reviewing your notes. Spend another 5 – 10 minutes one week later and a further 5 – 10 minutes a month later.
Total time for the book: 30 mins

This multi-step way of reading should enable you to comprehend a 250 page textbook at a very high level, with a total time expenditure of about 360 minutes, including making notes. (Approx six hours). That time includes a lot of active reading, note taking and subsequent reviewing.

This is about twice as fast as most untrained people would read a 250 page textbook **once**. Yet you would have reviewed the material at least four times, and taken visually memorable notes.

Speed read a book on car engines and you'll learn what the basic components are (manifold, carburettor, ignition, etc). That's valuable because then you'll want to know how they all fit together.

To understand how the car works, however, you need to slow down and see the relationships.

ACTION

Take a sizeable book you need to read. Apply the above method to it. Then compare your findings to the estimates above.

• Did the method help?

• How much faster did you read it?

• Was your understanding and memory improved?

State of mind is the first stage in learning. That's why we prefer the name Power Reading to speed reading. Speed reading implies you need to read fast all the time. Some people find that creates anxiety and pressure.

Power reading acknowledges that there are times when you do slow down. Speed is for scanning.

Some texts on new or complex subjects demand reading so it sounds in your head.

You will probably also need to stop frequently to consider the implications of what you are reading.

Summary

Power reading is an efficient way of searching for ideas without needing to read every word with equal attention.

Power read a book the way you read a timetable. Skim over all the irrelevant bits, then slow right down and pore over the part that's important for you. The part that tells you something you didn't know.

The question to ask before starting a book is, "What do I want from this?" Then the way you read becomes obvious. If it's a magazine or additional background reading, then a tripled rate of reading is a very valuable asset.

If you are reading a textbook, then speed reading is ideal for the scan part. When it comes to the core of your textbook, speed is not everything – though it's certain that you can read considerably faster than you have probably thought.

How fast you read depends on why you are reading. Power reading is variable speed reading.

M.A.S.T.E.R.
Acquire the Facts

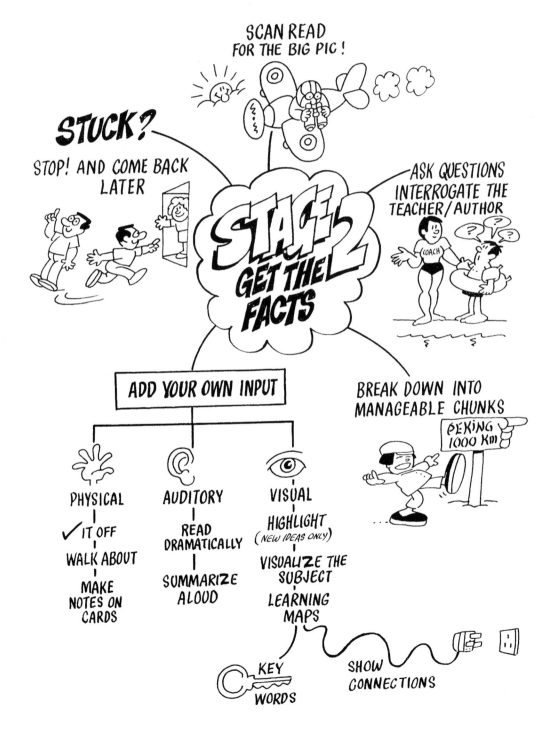

SCAN READ
FOR THE BIG PIC!

STUCK?
STOP! AND COME BACK
LATER

ASK QUESTIONS
INTERROGATE THE
TEACHER / AUTHOR

STAGE 2
GET THE
FACTS

ADD YOUR OWN INPUT

BREAK DOWN INTO
MANAGEABLE CHUNKS

PEKING
1000 KM

PHYSICAL

✓ IT OFF
WALK ABOUT
MAKE
NOTES ON
CARDS

AUDITORY

READ
DRAMATICALLY

SUMMARIZE
ALOUD

VISUAL

HIGHLIGHT
(NEW IDEAS ONLY)

VISUALIZE THE
SUBJECT

LEARNING
MAPS

KEY
WORDS

SHOW
CONNECTIONS

YOUR NOTES

"Active reading is a conversation with the author."
Consequently we invite you to use this page for notes and to ask yourself at least some of these questions.

What was the big idea? What was new?

What assumptions were made? Do I agree with them?

What was fact? Was the evidence reasonable? What was not clear?

What was opinion? Can I accept it? Was any issue oversimplified?

What are my main conclusions? What are the consequences?

How can I use what I've learned?   For my personal learning?   Training?   At home?

What do I want to explore further?

Stage 3
Search out the Meaning

Information isn't understanding

Unfortunately, we have all had the experience of something 'going in one ear and out the other'. That's because acquiring the basic facts is only the start of learning. It's entirely possible to know about something without understanding it. For me, electricity is a good example!

You can compare learning with a plant. When you first go over the subject, your knowledge of it is like a seedling – clinging precariously to the surface of the ground. Unless that seedling becomes a fully flowering plant, with strong and deep roots, it is all too easy for it to wither away.

To convert surface knowledge to deep learning, you have to **do** something to make it take root. Once you have got the basic facts, you have to stop and explore the subject.

This is where you can begin to use the full range of your EIGHT different intelligences.

Learning is not something that's done to you. **Only you can do it.** The best any trainer, author or teacher can do is provide an environment and materials that encourage you to want to explore and learn. And help you overcome difficulties. The actual business of learning is entirely **your** responsibility!

SURFACE KNOWLEDGE   **DEEP LEARNING**

BRAIN WORKOUT

Brains are like muscles. When you deliberately use your range of intelligences you exercise your brain.

Like your muscles, your brain power literally does grow with use. That's why intelligence is not fixed. You are an important influence on your own brain.

Your eight intelligences

Howard Gardner and colleagues at Harvard University have demonstrated that when people involve a range of intelligences, their learning ability is greatly enhanced.

Each type of intelligence represents a different way to explore the subject. A different ability to call on when you need to tackle a problem – although the naturalist intelligence is more useful to check the social or environmental effect of what you are learning.

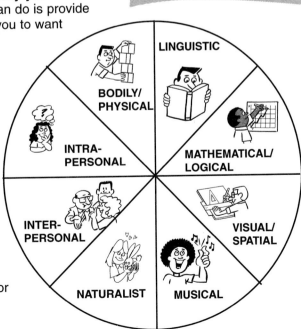

LINGUISTIC

BODILY/ PHYSICAL

INTRA- PERSONAL

MATHEMATICAL/ LOGICAL

INTER- PERSONAL

VISUAL/ SPATIAL

NATURALIST

MUSICAL

Use your full range
of intelligences

**EXPERIENCE IS
THE BEST TEACHER**

You learn more about a road
by travelling down it, than
from all the maps in the
world.

*THEORY INTO
KNOWLEDGE*

*If I were to tell you that an acre
is 4047 square metres, that's
data. Easily forgotten, because
it doesn't mean much.*

*If, instead, you were to discover
that an acre is about the size of
a football pitch, that's
knowledge. You have related it
to something you know.*

*You probably used your visual
intelligence by picturing a
football field.*

*You took something that was
just abstract information and
turned it into meaningful and
useful knowledge.*

*That is a pretty good definition
of learning!*

This new way of looking at intelligence tells us two critically
important things:

- **Intelligence is not fixed.** A person can excel in one
situation and appear to be highly intelligent. Yet he may
be at a complete loss in a different situation. The
absent-minded maths professor who cannot communicate
illustrates this well!

- **Intelligence is a set of abilities and skills.** It is
demonstrated by what people do and achieve.

This book describes a broad range of skills for learning. The
more tools of the learning trade an individual possesses, the
more flexible and competent a learner he is.

Consciously using your **full** range of intelligences leads to
balanced learning – learning that not only suits your current
strengths, but that also enables you to develop others. Using
your full range of intelligences will also prompt you to think in
new ways. And that's a good definition of creativity.

What are your strongest intelligences?

We've given you three separate ways to decide.

---

1 RECORD WHAT YOU FEEL THEY ARE

You do this by shading in those segments of the innermost
profile circle on page 57 that correspond to your strengths.
For example, somebody who considered she was strongest
in linguistic, musical and bodily/physical intelligences would
shade in the following segments of the innermost (first)
circle, eg:

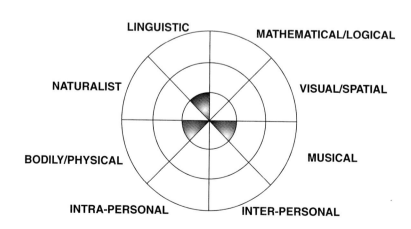

2 | WHAT STATEMENTS DESCRIBE YOU BEST?

Linguistic

- ○ Appreciates plays, poetry, books, radio, conversation – enjoys language
- ○ Learns well from books, tapes, lectures and listening to others
- ○ Fluent, expressive talker with well developed vocabulary
- ○ Good at explaining things
- ○ Likes to write things down

Mathematical/Logical

- ○ Likes logical explanations
- ○ Likes to solve puzzles and problems
- ○ Looks for patterns and relationships between things
- ○ Approaches tasks/problems in a logical, step-by-step manner

Visual/Spatial

- ○ Good sense of direction
- ○ Observant, sees things others do not notice
- ○ Can see things clearly in their mind's eye
- ○ Films, slides, videos help learning
- ○ Uses charts, diagrams, maps easily

Musical

- ○ Enjoys sounds in nature
- ○ Interested in music
- ○ Enjoys hearing and/or making music
- ○ Good sense of rhythm and/or melody
- ○ Readily learns and retains lyrics

Inter-personal

- ○ Can help with difficulties between people
- ○ Sensitive to others' moods and reactions
- ○ Interested in how others think and feel
- ○ Involved in clubs and/or community activity
- ○ Enjoys teamwork, discussing and co-operating with others

Intra-personal

- ○ Likes to daydream, imagine, fantasize
- ○ Enjoys doing things independently of others
- ○ Appreciates privacy and quiet for working and thinking
- ○ Understands their own feelings and thoughts and why they do things
- ○ Ponders on the relevance of what they are doing and draws conclusions from past experiences

Bodily/Physical

- ○ Likes to deal with problems physically, get directly involved, get 'hands on'
- ○ Skilful when working with things
- ○ Enjoys sports, games, physical exercise
- ○ Likes to be moving, doing or touching something they are learning about
- ○ Remembers best what they have done (as compared to seen or heard)

Naturalist

- ○ Can recognize and name many different types of plants, trees and flowers
- ○ Very conscious of, and actively supports, environmental issues
- ○ Feels an affinity to nature. Can imagine themselves as a farmer or fisherman
- ○ Can read weather signs and conscious of wildlife and tracks on a walk

INTELLIGENT IN DIFFERENT WAYS

The importance of Howard Gardner's theory is this. We've moved from "How smart are you?" to "How are you smart?" Each person is intelligent in different ways.

ACTION

Tick (✓) the ones that fairly describe you. The more you tick in any one area of intelligence the stronger you will tend to be in that intelligence.

When you've finished, transfer your strengths by shading in the appropriate intelligences in the middle ring on page 57.

3   WHAT ARE YOU GOOD AT?

Linguistic
- ○ Verbal arguments
- ○ Crosswords, word puzzles
- ○ Letter/report writing
- ○ Form filling
- ○ Finding information – from newspapers, brochures, books, etc
- ○ Verse, poetry
- ○ Giving clear explanations
- ○ Giving instructions
- ○ Writing

Mathematical/Logical
- ○ Budgeting
- ○ Family accounts
- ○ Planning journeys
- ○ Calculating scores
- ○ Calculating odds on bets
- ○ Estimating quantities
- ○ Managing/planning time, timetables
- ○ Mathematics
- ○ Science

Visual/Spatial
- ○ Map reading and navigating
- ○ Using diagrams and plans, eg: engine diagrams
- ○ Self-assembly furniture
- ○ Driving, parking
- ○ Planning gardens
- ○ Art
- ○ Dressmaking
- ○ Model layouts, eg: train sets and model making

Musical
- ○ Music making
- ○ Repeating songs you've heard
- ○ Keeping time with music
- ○ Recognizing tunes
- ○ Moving in time to music
- ○ Remembering slogans, raps, verses
- ○ Selecting appropriate music, eg: background music

Inter-personal
- ○ Listening carefully
- ○ Committee work
- ○ Managing/supervising others
- ○ Parenting – teaching, playing with, helping, consoling, managing children, young people
- ○ Helping others with personal problems
- ○ Youth work, sports clubs, etc
- ○ Teaching/training others

Intra-personal
- ○ Keeping a personal diary/journal
- ○ Predicting what you'll be able to do well or have difficulty with
- ○ Planning own time
- ○ Understanding your feelings and moods
- ○ Recognizing who you are like/unlike
- ○ Setting personal goals

Bodily/Physical
- ○ Sport
- ○ Dancing
- ○ Car maintenance
- ○ Do it yourself – carpentry, bricklaying, plastering, tiling, etc
- ○ Rough and tumble play with children
- ○ Hobbies involving delicate handiwork, eg: marquetry, model building, knitting, embroidery
- ○ Cooking, baking, cake decorating

Naturalist
- ○ Keeping up to date on the evolution of the universe, stars and life sciences
- ○ Making practical contributions to conservation issues
- ○ Gardening
- ○ Pet keeping

ACTION

Now transfer your conclusions to the Intelligence Profile on page 57, ie: shade in the segments which represent your current strengths in the outer circle which is labelled 'results from exploration 3'.

A current profile of your intelligences

Howard Gardner – who evolved the idea of multiple intelligence – makes a critically important point. Our schools (and training rooms) typically teach us to involve the linguistic and mathematical/logical intelligence. So if your brain is naturally set up to be good with words and figures, you will do well in formal education.

If you like a teaching style that reveals the subject bit by bit in a logical step-by-step manner, you will like the way most textbooks and lectures are put together.

But this approach – typical of formal teaching and learning – is mostly directed to just two types of intelligence, ie: 'linguistic' and 'mathematical/logical'.

If that's the way your brain naturally works, you're lucky. However, for people whose natural strengths are not linguistic or mathematical/logical, school may have been a tough experience, because it mostly offers a single chance to understand. What Howard Gardner calls 'the single chance theory of education'.

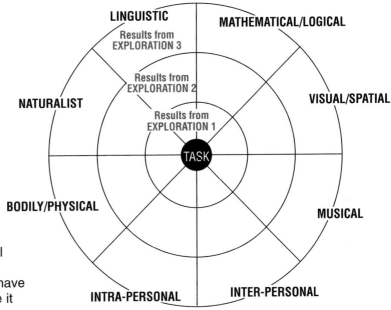

Multiple chance learning

People who prefer – and often **need** – other ways to explore a subject are not well served by the way we normally present information at school, in training rooms, or in text books. So they achieve less than they could. Yet give them the chance to also use other types of intelligence and they can blossom.

This is the 'multiple chance' theory of education and training.

When you are more aware of the unique make-up of your own brain and therefore know how to use it best, you can become a highly proficient learner.

When you are more aware of the variety of learning styles in others whom you have to instruct, you become a better communicator. And when you become aware of your children's learning styles, you become better able to understand and help their learning. Most people can learn anything – given only time.

MAKE SENSE?

- Does this help explain people's feelings towards school and learning?
- What relevance does this have to me and my family?
- How can I use this information?

___

"A mind stretched to a new idea never returns to its original dimension."

Oliver Wendell Holmes

___

"When everyone thinks alike – nobody thinks much."

Dee Dickinson

Using mathematical/logical intelligence

Rate or list the key points and number them

Choosing the important points of a subject means think carefully about what you are learning.

You can't rank the points without comparing them and you can't compare them without considering the relative significance of each point. That requires depth of thought.

Analyze what you are learning

When you are systematic, you use your logical intelligence. When you are analytical, you also use your logical intelligence! So when you use **a system** to be **analytical**, you are **really** using your logical intelligence!

When you analyze what you are learning, you don't take it at face value, you explore it in depth. And that's effective learning. The following A.E.I.O.U. systematic approach helps.

A   What ASSUMPTIONS are being made?

Has anything been taken for granted? Has anything been left out? Has the author used an isolated example to make a general sweeping conclusion?

E   What's the EVIDENCE for this?

Are we dealing with facts or opinion? If it's opinion – can I trust the source? If it's fact – is this always true? What other explanations can there be? If this is true, what else follows?

I   Can I think of a good ILLUSTRATION or example of this?

Does this fit in with anything else I'm familiar with? Is what I'm reading or hearing consistent with my experience?

O   What OPINION or conclusions can I draw about this?

Are they justified?

U   What are the UNIQUE points in this?

What are the key and new points? What is essential to know – and what is just padding?

Make a flow chart or diagram that expresses what you are learning in a step-by-step manner

Again, the thought that goes into such an activity ensures you really begin to understand the subject.

SYSTEMS MAKE LIFE EASIER

The value of a systematic approach is that it makes life easier. You know that if you follow the plan you will achieve a good result. A bit like assembling a model from a kit or painting by numbers!

Applying your logical intelligence to this book could also involve:

- *Trying out each of the ideas in this section and grading them to establish which combinations seem to suit you best.*

- *Listing the key points of the book and sorting them into a logical sequence. (We do that on page 119. Contrast it with the summary on page 118.)*

Which do you prefer?

LEARNING NEEDS THINKING!

The A.E.I.O.U. questions help make sure you always stop and think. Your initial conclusions may not always be right.

What's more, authors, teachers and trainers are human. They are not always right either!

If you are not asking questions, you are probably not learning!

Using your linguistic intelligence

Put it into your own words

It is hard work to learn words written by somebody else. Which is why it's difficult to learn a poem or the lines of a play. Learning the words parrot-fashion certainly does not mean you understand them. But to put what you have heard or read into your own words, **does** require you to understand it.

Brainstorm from memory all the things you feel you have learned. Write them down or say them into a tape recorder.

Next, skim through the pages of the book to jog your memory and add further thoughts. Be careful to put these into your own words – don't copy out or merely repeat chunks of the text.

You will now have a list of points. You can next organize these points in any way that is meaningful to you, eg: you can select the five most important points, and put them on post cards.

When you are reading, stop at the end of each main section, lay your book aside and recall the key ideas in your own words from memory

Then, if relevant, put your conclusions into your own words.

Jot down the questions that arise from what you've learned

Then find the answers and express them aloud.

Using your intra-personal intelligence

Look for personal significance

What is your favourite hobby? Nobody had to push you to learn it. If you are interested in a subject, you're motivated to learn. But what if you are faced with a subject that currently seems boring?

Researchers tested students' memory for paintings. Some just looked at the paintings, others were given information about the painting and the painter. The latter group remembered the paintings twice as well.

They remembered better because they created their own interest in the subject by digging deeper. They explored the subject on a **personal level**.

So whatever the subject, investigate the background – especially the human interest. If the subject were art, music or drama, what was in the creator's mind? What did she or he do differently from anyone else before? What new technique did she evolve?

You need words in order to think. If children lack an adequate vocabulary they are forced to express themselves in other ways.

Sometimes they hit out at the world, because they feel they have no other way to communicate than physically.

That's why reading to young children and conversation is so important. TV is a passive medium which uses mainly dialogue and rarely needs descriptive language because the viewer can see what's going on.

It cannot, therefore, give the depth of language skills that reading provides.

DIARIES FOR SUCCESS

If you go into any library, you will find that a remarkable number of successful people kept diaries and journals and wrote detailed letters to their family and friends.

Researcher Dr Win Wenger poses a question, "Did these outstanding people record their observation of things from early childhood because they knew that some day they were going to be great?

"Or did the practice of recording their own observations develop in them the characteristics which led to their becoming great?"

Worth thinking about!

If world population is growing at 2% per year – how many years will it take before the total population doubles?

Quick answer 35 years.

Why? Because there is a simple, useful maths rule. Divide any percentage rate of growth into 70 to find the time it takes for something to double. So:

70 ÷ 2 = 35

World population was almost 6,000,000,000 people (ie: almost six billion people) in 1998.

If it were to grow at 3% rather than 2%, then the time it would take for our planet to have to accommodate yet another six billion people would be just over 23 years.

So by the year 2020 the world population would, on average, be increasing by over 200 million people a year.

That's the equivalent of a new France and Germany – every year!

When statistics start with a question of personal interest, the subject holds your attention. Just look at the margin. The same advice applies to technical subjects at work. Look for the human interest. Who developed the system? What were their initial difficulties and failures? Why is the system designed the way it is?

Once you've hit on the personal significance, genuine interest follows. People, the unusual, and unexpected connections make subjects interesting.

Above all we become interested when we can answer the question "Why does this matter to **me**?"

Make time for reflection

Take time quietly to reflect on the subject – how does it fit in with what you know already? How does it relate to your past experience? How can it benefit you in the future?

When you are learning anything, a good strategy is to find a way to compare what's new with what's familiar.

For example, a carburettor works in a similar way to a perfume spray. The perfume spray sucks up both the liquid and air at the same time. Then it blows the mixture out together in a fine mist.

A carburettor sucks up petrol and air together and also blows them out in a fine mist which is then burned to produce energy.

The more real or 'concrete' you make something that is new, the better you understand it. An everyday comparison is a good way to make it real.

Using your visual/spatial intelligence

Creating a learning map

Throughout this book we have summarized the information we have given to you on learning maps. These are even more helpful aids to learning when you have constructed them yourself.

Make a large learning map which summarizes all that you have learned until now. You will be able to add further information as you read on.

Sometimes all you need is a brief sketch. Many mathematical concepts are easier to solve when you find a way to diagram them.

Try the bookworm problem in the margin opposite now.

There are **lots** of ways to explore a subject visually. Depending on appropriateness, consider making up a coloured poster, a diagram, or a time line. Use symbols instead of words. Colour code your work.

Create an image

Create a strong visual image of what you are trying to learn in your mind's eye. A sort of mental TV documentary.

Often it's the only way to really understand a process that takes place inside a piece of equipment – a printed circuit board, for example, or a new chemical process.

Imagery's **so** powerful we've highlighted it as a Super Skill on p.68.

Using your inter-personal intelligence

Teach what you've learned

The best way to learn **is** to teach. Because when you take time to explain what you've learned to someone else you'll rapidly discover if you really understand it – or if you only thought you understood it!

Teaching requires you to collect your thoughts in logical order and put the ideas into your own words.

Moreover you gain from the other person's experiences and insights, especially if they ask you questions and even challenge your opinions.

Compare notes

The simple act of comparing notes at the end of a lecture or a book with a friend or with colleagues will always surprise you. They will have understood or remembered things you didn't, and vice versa. You also see the different ways they approached the task – and you therefore learn about other learning styles.

Involve your children

Ask your children what they think of some ideas in this book. Let them tell you their feelings and experiences about learning. Do they get on well in a particular class? Why is that? Does the way it's taught match the way they like to learn? Do they find these ideas useful?

Inter-personal (or co-operative) learning is so important that we rate it as a Super Skill – examined on page 73.

THE BOOKWORM

Four volumes of an encyclopedia stand side-by-side on a shelf, the correct way round. Volume I is on the left, Volume IV is on the right.

Each book is 100 mm thick and the covers are 5 mm thick.

A bookworm starts eating at page one of Volume I, and eats its way through to the last page of Volume IV.

How many millimetres did it chew through?

Answer on page 72.

WE'RE SOCIAL LEARNERS

It's easy to think you understand something, but when you have to explain it to someone else, it forces you to clear up any 'woolly' thoughts.

What's more, learning with others is usually more enjoyable. Their questions and insights also bring a fresh viewpoint to the subject.

You use your inter-personal intelligence when you consider how this book could help your company, your family, your school or your community.

Learning action circles

Here's an idea to speed learning around your organization.

Decide on a topic that you all agree will make your work more efficient. Say it was Quality Management and there were six people in your group. You each select a book or video, or training programme on the subject, and agree to meet in, say, one month.

You each summarize what you've learned for the others. Result? Six approaches are learned and adapted to your own company's circumstances in the time it might take for an individual to comprehend two.

Using your bodily/physical intelligence

Role play

Many people can't think for long while they are sitting still. Acting out something that you are learning allows you to turn theory into something more memorable.

Role play helps you explore a new approach or skill in a safe situation. It also helps you see the world from another's point of view.

For example, people will learn more about the importance of easy access for the disabled by trying to negotiate a building in a wheelchair, or by wearing glasses smeared with vaseline to simulate poor vision, than from any number of brochures.

Acting out words and phrases when you are learning a foreign language is very effective, because you **physically** register the language in your memory.

The power of writing

Writing is a physical exercise, so we should not be surprised that when we write something down, we learn it better. We have added a physical element (writing), to sight (reading), and sound (inner speech).

Sort your thoughts

Make up post cards of the main points of what you've learned and sort them out in a logical order. You can also carry these flash cards with you and revise with them from time to time. Or pin them on a notice board to remind you.

When you make notes on cards to pin up or carry with you, you are not only physically engaged in writing, but the handling and sorting of the cards makes the information easier to remember.

"An ounce of experience is worth a ton of theory."

Benjamin Franklin

STUDDY BUDDY

Here's a proven way to learn better.

a. Team up with a colleague.

b. You each agree to learn the same chapter or section independently.

c. When you next meet, you both summarize what you have learned to each other and discuss differing interpretations.

You both learn better!

There are lots of ways physically to explore a subject.

If you were trying to explain this book to a child, you could make up a sheet with all the tools of learning on it, and then cut it out to make a jigsaw.

By assembling the jigsaw, the child would see how the elements all 'fitted together'.

Musical exploration

Write a song, jingle, poem or rap

Do you find remembering the lyrics of a song or an advertising jingle easier than remembering a piece of text?

Think how many songs you know – yet have never consciously learned.

Some of the most memorable advertising messages are presented in jingles, and years later you still remember them. And it is through rhyme that we remember the days in each month – "Thirty days hath September", etc.

When you express what you want to say in a concise and rhythmic way, and then fit those words to a melody, it makes the words highly memorable, because you have to really think about what you are learning in order to do this.

Background music

Music stimulates the emotional centre of our brain and our emotions are strongly linked to our long-term memory. So playing some background music as you learn – especially quiet classical music – has proved to be very effective for many people.

Modern technology allows us to see which areas of the brain are working at any one time. The **same** area of the brain is functioning when someone is engaged in mathematical reasoning as when they are performing and reading music.

Research from test schools indicates that when one hour a day of music, art and drama is added to the timetable, grades in ALL the other subjects can be improved by as much as 20%. Active involvement in music and the arts is a **centrally** important element in raising confidence, enjoyment and actual grade standards in schools. But are we taking enough notice of this fact?

Estate agents have to learn complex new European rules. One enterprising exam candidate set the rules to music and she passed top of her class.

CHANTING TO SUCCESS

Learning and singing songs in a foreign language is an effective and pleasant way to expand your vocabulary.

Singing or chanting mathematical or scientific formulae works well too.

Music is a much more powerful learning aid than we normally appreciate.

DEVELOP THINKING THROUGH THE ARTS

When you study the arts you develop your ability to perceive and think in new ways.

The arts are forms of communication – so you develop skills of interpretation. They provide insight and wisdom, not just information.

Learning through the arts builds the inner spirit as well as the brain and our understanding of human values.

"The impossible is often the untried."

Jim Goodwin

TRAINING TIPS

Helping them search out the meaning

This stage is the heart of the training session – where trainees or students turn raw facts into personal understanding.

You'll want to accommodate differing learning styles, so the aim is to create a cycle of activities based on a range of intelligences. That way you are not only reaching the widest possible audience – but they also have several chances to understand the same information. You achieve breadth and depth.

"What would you attempt to do, if you knew you could not fail?"

Dr Robert Schüller

Create a checklist of activities that you think will help different types of learners to really explore and understand the subject based on the multiple intelligences. It's natural to want to teach in the way we learn. A checklist helps guard against the natural, but wrong assumption, that other people learn the way you do.

Look back at the various learning strategies and work out some teaching strategies that match them. Here are just a few of the ideas that we have found work well.

Linguistic

- **Flash cards:** Ask the group to prepare flash cards that summarize the main points of what they have learned.

   Ask them to create an advertising poster for what they have learned.

- **Add on:** Sit the group in a circle and give each member a number in sequence. Trainee Number 1 starts off by summarizing an element of what they have learned in a sentence. She then calls out a number.

   The trainee who is that number then summarizes or repeats the first sentence and adds one of her own, finishing by calling out a new number. Each new trainee only summarizes the immediately preceding sentence, before adding his own. Works well to learn, for example, the features of a new product line.

Logical/Mathematical

- **Rank it:** Ask trainees to take the points they have learned and not only number them, but rank them in order of importance. To rank a series of points you have to really think about and compare them – and that requires depth of thought, which is learning.

- **Flow chart:** Ask them to create a flow chart of the order in which things are done.

- **Group memory flashing:** Divide the group into teams of three or four. Give each group a part of the day's lesson content to summarize on a learning map. Together the individual maps will make up the whole day's learning. Then have each group present their map to the room on a flip chart.

  This learning map is now covered up and the whole group must reproduce it from memory. Compare the original and the new maps and add any missing elements. Repeat this until all the maps have been presented and reproduced.

  The result is that the whole group has been actively involved in a very visual and physical way. You can be sure they'll remember the session!

- **TV documentary:** Create groups and task each group to become a team of TV directors. Their job is to produce an exciting TV documentary of what they have learned from the day's session. Money no object! Have each group present their story board and then hold an Academy Award Ceremony.

Visual/Spatial

- **Create a rap:** Or limerick, jingle or rhyme to summarize a part or even all of what's been learned. Could they take a nursery rhyme and substitute the old words with the important ideas from what they're learning?

  Like all these activities, it's the concentration and thought that the activity provokes – rather than the actual result – that ensures that effective learning takes place.

Musical

- **Problem swap:** Create groups of about five. Each group then has to agree on a problem in the business that they would like solved. They write it on a card and then the cards are swapped. The new group tries to find and agree on a solution. This is an excellent technique that develops a habit of informal team problem solving.

  You will find that all aspects of training are improved and enjoyed more when you get people working together in teams. For this reason there is a section on co-operative learning on page 73.

Inter-personal

- **Explain to others:** Ask them to imagine going home and explaining to their family how they will use today's information in their own lives.

Intra-personal

Bodily/Physical

- **Role play:** Whilst role play can be very effective, it can also be stressful for the people involved who are watched.

  A good way to remove the stress is to ask the observers to advise the role players on how to carry out their task. Then the observers' job is to evaluate how well their advice is working, rather than the performance of the players – who therefore have much less pressure on them. Good for sales training.

- **Sequence shuffle:** If they are learning a process, have each member make up a card with part of the sequence or system on it. Trainees then come up in the proper order and explain their part of the sequence. At the end they will have physically arranged themselves in the correct order of the process.

  Works well to learn, eg: a production process, banking procedure, steps in an application or administrative sequence.

Naturalist

- **A naturalist intelligence:** This is a universal human talent, but it is not, for most people, an obvious intelligence to use for general learning. Use it more as a reminder to check on the social or environmental effects of what you are learning.

PARENT TIPS

Helping her create meaning from data

All the ideas in this section can be used by or adapted for even quite young children.

Encourage her to explain, informally, what she's learning to you. It helps her clarify her thoughts. But don't, of course, turn your home into a second school! Nothing is better calculated to turn her off.

One thing that you can do that is always popular and successful is to look for ways you can role-play concepts. Children relate best to concrete examples, not theory. Here are two examples to spark off your own ideas.

Why do metals expand when they get hot?

Get three or four of the family to stand close together. That represents atoms that are cold and packed close together. Now jiggle up and down. That represents atoms that have been heated and are more active. You – and they – now take up more space. That's why metal expands.

How does the moon cause the tides?

Roll down the sleeve of your shirt. Then explain that a large mass creates a gravitational pull. So when the moon (a large mass) travels across an ocean it pulls the water upwards in the middle of the ocean.

As you say this, use your fist to represent the moon and when it gets to the middle of your other arm pluck your sleeve upwards. Show your child that the end of your sleeve has now moved up your arm. That represents the tide going out.

Of course when the moon has reached the other side of the ocean and is now moving over land, the pull of gravity is reduced and the 'hump' of water goes down. This extra water now flows back to the coast-line. Release your sleeve and your cuff will now move back towards your hand. The 'tide' has come in. It's more dramatic and memorable than any amount of theory.

Invite the whole family to come up with ideas that make abstract concepts real.

YOUR ROLE

Your role is to fill in a gap in our educational system, which is that very few schools teach learning strategies.

In an interesting experiment in Canada, one group of students was given a list of French words to learn. The other group was merely asked to sort the French words out into nouns, verbs and adjectives.

The group who sorted learned more than the group who deliberately tried to learn!

Because they were having to think about each word in depth to categorize it.

SUPER SKILL 2

Using imagery

At the beginning of the 20th century, Einstein began to realize that Isaac Newton's theory of gravity had inconsistencies in it. One day, relaxing and daydreaming, he pictured himself inside an elevator that was hurtling through space, faster than the speed of light. He visualized a small opening on one side of the elevator wall. A beam of light shone through this opening and was projected onto the opposite wall.

"The interaction of images is the source of thought. The words of the language, as they are written or spoken, do not seem to play any role in my mechanism of thought."

Albert Einstein

The fact that gravity could bend light remained a theory until scientists were able to make precise measurements during an eclipse. They then proved that the light from a distant star was indeed bent into a curve by the huge gravitational pull of the sun.

Suddenly he realized that, if the elevator was moving upwards sufficiently fast, it would travel far enough in that split second so that an observer inside would see the beam of light as curved. From this 'insight that transcends logic', Einstein concluded that gravity is able to bend light.

There are other examples of vital discoveries that did not come from logic alone. Insights that needed visual inspiration.

The German organic chemist, Friedrich Kekule, was trying to imagine how the chemical structure of benzene might appear. As he closed his eyes by the fire, a vision of a snake chasing its tail came into his mind. He suddenly realized that the atomic structure of benzene might take the form of a closed ring. It is estimated that almost 60% of all organic chemistry was triggered by the insight of that daydream!

Imagery and visualization (the terms are interchangeable), can be one of your most powerful learning and training strategies.

The basis of imagery

The terms imagery or visualization imply that you will only use your inner visual sense. That's not so. A chef has an image of how the meal will taste. A composer has an image of how the music will sound. And you have an image of how it will feel to kiss a loved one. In fact, if you didn't make pictures in your head of how wonderful something was going to be, you would never get disappointed!

IMAGINATION

"Imagination is more important than knowledge for while knowledge points to all there is, imagination points to all there will be."

Albert Einstein

The strongest and most useful imagery uses as many of the senses as possible. You will want to see the subject in your mind's eye, to hear it and to feel or sense it. You did that when you 'visualized' the taste of a lemon.

Imagery works so well because, as the philosopher Kant said, "Thinking in pictures precedes thinking in words". We mostly think in images and then express those thoughts in words. So, in one sense, words are only a second-hand representation of your experiences. They can never exactly convey what you actually feel.

One important proviso. It is a mistake to think that imagery only works when you see clear pictures. Many people do not see clear pictures initially, and yet can gain all the benefits of the guided imagery technique explained below.

Be there. Be it.

There are two ways in which we visualize something. We can either visualize the subject with our feelings attached – or as a detached observer. Two short descriptions will demonstrate the difference.

> **EVERYONE HAS THE POWER TO VISUALIZE**
>
> Have you ever worried about something? Worry is merely the process whereby you picture something unpleasant and 'feel' as if it's already happened.
>
> If you can worry – you can visualize!

Detached

Imagine you are at a big fairground. The roller-coaster ride is some 100 yards away. You look at the crisscross supports that surround the roller-coaster and see how the roller-coaster track rises and falls inside.

Just then you notice, even at this distance, that the little roller-coaster train is full of people, chugging slowly up the steep track that forms the first part of the ride. The train reaches the top, halts for a second, and then starts to descend rapidly into the first loop. You hear the passengers shout and scream in the distance.

Involved

You are at the same fairground. Now, however, you have paid for the roller-coaster ride. You walk over and sit in the very front car of the train. Your hands reach out and grip the iron rail in front of you, which is cool in the early evening air.

The train jolts and moves slowly up the pinion track. You gaze upwards and the track stretches steeply ahead. A smell of fried onions from the hamburger and hot dog stand drifts upwards.

The car clanks up the track. You can see the top of the track, dark against the blue evening sky. The top is getting closer and closer, and all around you people are giggling and oohing nervously.

The roller-coaster car reaches the very top of the track, hundreds of feet in the air. You are vaguely conscious of the lights of the fairground below, but your eyes are rivetted on the huge, almost vertical, drop below you. Your knuckles are white where you grip the bar, your heart is pounding and your stomach tenses with anticipation.

The roller-coaster rocks for a second on the edge of the drop.

Then suddenly it plunges forward and down with a great clattering roar. Your back is pressed hard against the seat and the pit of your stomach feels as if it's been left way behind. The wind is sharp in your face, your hair blows backwards. You hear your own shouts mingling with the shrieks and screams of your fellow passengers.

Do you notice the difference between the two descriptions? In the first, you see the scene in a detached way. As an observer, with no special feelings or emotions. We call it **disassociated.**

In the second, you experience the scene from your own eyes, with all its **associated** feelings and sensations.

Imagery is most effective for learning if it uses all the senses, and you are there. The rule is 'Be there'. 'Be it.'

By using multi–sensory, **associated**, imagery you ensure that you interact with the subject you are learning, and you involve your emotional brain – a vital controller of your long-term memory.

Six steps to create your own imagery

Here is a six step process to make imagery work for you as a learning tool. Practise it regularly, and it becomes a very quick process.

1   Relax.

2   Breathe deeply.

3   Focus quietly. Close your eyes, if it helps.

4   Use multi-sensory associated imagery of the subject. **Be there**.

5   Complete the imagery by creating a learning map or making a drawing.

6   Finally, allow a few quiet moments to let any insight or intuition surface.

One important tip about imagery. Detail is what counts. So put foreground and background into your mental picture. Try your hardest to get movement into it and create some interactions in your image.

Everyone has the power to experience and use imagery. To prove that, take each of the following images and make a mental picture of them now. See the image, hear the sounds, feel the sensations. You will soon recognize you have the power!

- Imagine yourself scratching your finger nails on a blackboard.

- Imagine the sight, sound and feeling of a fountain playing in a sunlit courtyard.

- Imagine a really wet dog shaking himself.

- Imagine the smell of a rose.

- Imagine stroking a cat.

- Imagine the sound of your favourite rock band.

- Imagine wiggling your toes on grass, wet with morning dew.

- Imagine looking down from the roof of a huge skyscraper with the traffic, looking like toy cars, far below.

---

*The Force was
with her*

Olympic pentathlete, Marilyn King, is testimony to the power of imagery.

She had trained hard for three years, and there was about one more year before the Olympics. Then, just as she should have been gearing up to a peak before the Olympic trials in eight months' time, she had a car accident. She was laid up on her back in hospital for six months.

Lacking any opportunity for physical training, she practised her routines over and over in her mind. Day after day, she 'exercised' using imagery.

When she eventually left hospital, she had just two months to get fit for the Pentathlon – one of the most gruelling events in the Olympics.

At her first physical try-out her coach was astonished. Her muscles and fitness were at such a level that she was able to bring herself to peak performance within four weeks of leaving hospital. Her mind had literally trained and toned her body.

She not only succeeded in passing the trials, she succeeded at the Olympics themselves.

Today Marilyn King coaches 'at risk' children in using imagery to develop their true potential.

Thinking about the wet dog for a moment, what sort of dog was it? What colour? Did it shake more at the rear than at the front? Did you see its teeth?

You could not have answered any of these questions if you had not 'seen' the dog in your mind's eye.

Learning and teaching with imagery

You can use imagery to learn or teach any subject. There's an example below. I have chosen science because it's quite close to a business environment without being too specific an example. So you see the principle involved. The whole power of using imagery comes from the fact that your visualization is personal to **you.** So the example will not be as effective as your own images – but it gives you a guide.

Let's say you were studying the structure of matter. Imagine you were in charge of a TV documentary on the subject. Your job is to interest the viewers, so naturally you want to make the most fascinating film possible – an award winning video!

Really let rip with this bit of imagery. After all, this is to be a TV documentary with no normal limits. You can interview people from the past, you can take your camera right inside an atom, film an electron, animate atoms combining to form molecules. You can even assemble a panel of experts who could never have met in real life.

One big advantage of the TV documentary approach to imagery is that there will be parts of the story that you find difficult to explain, that are unclear. There may even be blanks in your story. These are precisely the areas of knowledge that you need to fill in.

Take a tip from the professional film makers. Before they shoot a film, they produce a story board. A story board is a sequence of sketches. Each sketch represents a scene. In this way they can plan out how the film will look in advance.

You can produce an outline plan of the subject you are studying on a preliminary learning map. That tells you where you need more detail.

Now it's your turn ...

I hope that this example sparks off your own ideas for using visualization for a learning or training task. And how visualization is made 'real' through the idea of a mental TV documentary.

The best way to learn and understand **is** to teach. So, if you puzzle out how you would present your knowledge on a subject so that **other** people would find it interesting and understandable, you will come to really understand it yourself.

PEAK PERFORMERS

Dr Charles Garfield worked for years with astronauts at N.A.S.A.

He watched them rehearse every single operation again and again in simulators.

Later, he made a full time study of 'peak performers' – people who were world class experts in what they did.

What struck him was that they too used simulation – but their form of simulation was mental rehearsal.

They all used imagery to help them succeed.

NOW YOU!

Take a subject you need to learn – or part of a subject. Now think through how you would use imagery to learn that subject.

Most training courses lend themselves to imagery.

Try to build up a picture of an ideal performance in that aspect of your job. When you are happy with that performance replay the imagery over and over in your head. It builds not only performance but confidence.

Use imagery before job interviews, presentations or speeches to master not only the content but also the style.

Acting as an imaginary TV documentary maker is a strong idea. It ensures you look for imaginative ways to register the information. You'll look for pictures, sound and graphics. These are all powerful memory devices.

Sharpening up your skill with imagery

The following two exercises are simple, and you can do them anywhere. On public transport or at an odd moment. See how good you can become at manipulating mental images.

Colour change

Close your eyes and take a long slow deep breath. Put your finger and thumb together and say, "calm".

As you breathe out, picture a red circle in front of you. If it helps, picture that circle on the inside of the middle of your forehead.

Now change the circle to blue.

Now change the blue circle to yellow.

Now change the yellow circle to green.

Now put a white spot in the middle of your green circle.

Now change the white spot to a white line horizontally across the circle.

Now make the line revolve slowly.

Now stop the line and make it fade.

An apple a day

Picture an apple on the movie screen of your mind.

Then add a second apple.

Now a third.

Now a fourth.

Now make it five.

Examine these five apples and see if they are all the same colour. Are they all the same shape? Do any move? Is the skin shiny? Do any have stalks or leaves on them?

Now see how they are arranged. Are they dotted about? Or all in a row? Or in a circle?

Finally open your eyes and draw the apples in exactly the same position as they were in your head.

THE BOOKWORM

Answer From page 61

The clue was that the problem occurred in the section on visual/spatial exploration. Most people answer 430 mm (4 x 100 mm books + 6 x 5 mm covers) because they apply their mathematical/logical intelligence straight away. In fact the answer is 230 mm. The picture shows why.

When the books are on the shelf, page one of Volume I is on the inside of the row of four books – not as you would assume, on the outside. Similarly, the last page of Volume IV is on the inside edge of that book. (See arrows.) So the bookworm only chews through two books and six covers!

Although the problem is trivial, it illustrates an important principle. Many problems need a creative solution that lies outside simple logic. Often visualization is a key to unlock such a solution.

SUPER SKILL 3

Co-operative learning

Humans have become the earth's most successful species, not because of their competitiveness, but because of their talent for co-operation.

Economic wealth in our society depends on the creation of co-operative enterprises, which we call companies. Yet too often the conventional model for education is individual effort and competition.

That's a mistake because in the real world what matters (and what is rewarded) are team-work, good communication, division of labour and leadership skills. It's also the foundation of a happy social and family life. But we don't structure our education that way!

Most sports are based on team skills. Why should learning be different? Co-operative learning is invaluable because it not only helps the people involved understand the subject better, it also develops important social skills.

Co-operative learning can also be very ineffective! True co-operative learning is not simply sitting together talking, nor does it work if one person does all the work. It needs a proper structure to be effective.

The advice below helps you contribute to that structure either as a member of the group yourself or perhaps someone who is setting up the basis of a learning organization.

David and Roger Johnson of the University of Minnesota have vast experience of co-operative learning. They identify the following elements that need to exist for it to be truly effective.

Members must be inter-dependent

If you are a member of a co-operative learning or study group your responsibility is twofold – to learn yourself and to ensure that others learn too.

For this to work, your efforts must be essential to the group's success. In turn their efforts must contribute to your success in such a way that, without them, you can't succeed. In other words 'you sink or swim together'. When one succeeds you all succeed and when the group succeeds, you succeed.

"We must learn to live together as brothers, or perish together as fools."
David Lewis

COLLECTIVE INTELLIGENCE

"None of us is as smart as all of us."
David & Roger Johnson

"I never got very far until I stopped thinking I had to do everything myself."
F W Woolworth

This is what inter-dependence means. Unless this key element exists, you are not working co-operatively – you are working 'alone in a group'.

Some ways to achieve inter-dependence are:

Assign roles

One member of a group, for example, **reads** the material, and one is responsible for **recording** ideas and answers. Another member is responsible for **testing** that everyone does understand the subject.

THE SCEPTIC ROLE

"Have we made any assumptions that may not be true?"

"Have we explored all the possibilities?"

"Is this the only answer?"

"Have we double-checked our answers?"

The A.E.I.O.U. checklist on page 58 is a good guide too.

Other good roles include the **observer** – how effective is the group, how could it collaborate better? Or the **sceptic** – someone whose role would be to ask the sorts of questions listed in the margin.

Obviously you can rotate the roles from session to session and task to task.

Compare notes

Your partners will have picked up points you missed and vice versa. You can use this simple co-operative idea at the end of any class.

Break up the learning task into sections

If your group is of three people you each take a third, learn it thoroughly and then teach your section to the others.

Then you test each other out on your knowledge until you are all satisfied that each one of you has mastered the subject.

"People become lonely because they build walls instead of bridges."

Joseph Newton

Share answers

You each make up your own answers, share them, discuss them and finally agree on a best consensus answer. Even if the final reports are individual, rather than collective, it doesn't mean you can't edit each other's work or comment constructively on it.

In fact discussing and editing each other's work is a major function of a co-operative learning group.

Mixed groups work best

Whilst the usual aim of your group is a consensus, minority opinions should always be respected and recorded.

Small groups of different learning styles and abilities produce better and more creative work. The essence of the idea of multiple intelligence is that we all bring a unique perspective to each task and can learn from each other's strengths.

Agree on a clear objective for your group

Your overall objective as a group is to make sure that each one understands the subject or can do what is required. So not only would group members teach what they know to each other, but you would typically test each other, and edit each other's work.

A good way to create a clear group goal is to agree on a minimum standard that each individual in the group will achieve. This not only raises the performance of the initially weaker members, it also helps the stronger members – since the best way to learn is to teach.

Change your leader often

If the nature of the group calls for a leader, make sure that the leadership role is rotated. People only feel committed to a group if they participate and feel they have contributed.

To ensure that one person doesn't continually dominate the discussion, you might agree in advance on a maximum number of times each person could talk per session.

Make time to reflect

Ensure that you allocate a few minutes before the end of each co-operative group session when you can assess how well the collaboration worked – so you can learn how to do better in future.

The simple questions to ask are:

- What went well?
- What could have gone better?

The purpose of co-operative learning is not only to solve a problem or to learn something, it is also to learn the skills (and enjoyment) of working informally in a team.

These few minutes of reflection on the process of co-operation help you build the skills of collaboration that are vital for success in all aspects of life.

Keep the group together

Generally a group that has formed together to learn co-operatively should stay together for several projects.

You then begin to build a shared identity and you will often want to celebrate your successes together – both of which create further enjoyment. You may well want to give your team a name, for example.

"All for one, one for all."

Alexandre Dumas
The Three Musketeers

SHARE THE WORKLOAD

If the co-operation is related to a project, a good way to share the workload would be for each member of the group to track down sources, materials and references, and then present their research for group use.

That's the idea behind learning action circles.

One of the happiest feelings is to experience the power of a team. Many things that really are impossible for one person to achieve acting alone, are possible for a group acting together. Moreover, you begin to identify and respect qualities in other people which you never saw before – and they in turn come to respect your abilities.

Compete with other groups sometimes

Co-operation does not rule out competition with other groups, when that is feasible. A very enjoyable game is what we call 'Challenge Match'.

You take a textbook that you have all been learning and allocate, say, 40 minutes. Your team's task is to spend the first 20 minutes in dreaming up 10 questions, based on the textbook, that you feel will stump the opposing team. They have the same task, ie: to devise 10 questions to stump your team.

LOUD MOUTH!

Here's a way to have fun and make something really memorable.

Each one of your group goes into a corner. Then, in turn, you call out whatever you need to remember. You call out as if you were each on separate mountain tops, calling across a valley.

Silly? Perhaps!

Memorable? Absolutely!

Then you get together and ask each other your 10 prepared questions. If the textbook is very technical, you can each retain the book but allow only 15 seconds to find the answer.

Result? You can turn the learning, revision and testing of a potentially dull textbook into an energetic game.

I have a dollar.
You have a dollar.
We swap and neither
is better off.

But if I have an idea and
you have an idea
and we swap,
we are both richer.

SUPER SKILL 4

Clear communication

Co-operative learning involves collaboration and therefore the skill of communication. Such skills are not automatic, even though they are of huge value throughout life.

Good communication is rather like using a walkie-talkie set. That means:

1   You have to listen with complete attention in order to hear what's been said.

2   You cannot talk and listen at the same time!

3   You have to be broadcasting on the same wavelength!

Listen in order to interpret the whole meaning

How often have you been talking to someone, when their eyes moved elsewhere and they began to fidget? They were no longer listening – they were waiting for a gap in the conversation to make their point. They weren't trying to understand your point of view – they were waiting to reply with theirs.

There is a skill in listening in order to understand. You need to listen on **two** levels. At the level of words and at the level of feelings.

If the estimates in the side column are true, then listening for feelings is very important indeed – 80% of communication is non-verbal. So how do you make sure you have interpreted what the other person is **really** saying?

You ask in a way that makes it safe for the other person to express their feelings as well as the facts. So you listen closely to what they say, and how they say it. Then, like a true interpreter, you restate what you think they said.

Use a phrase like, "I want to make sure that I really understand how you **feel** about this. If I understand you correctly, you mean that …"

People communicate on two levels. Unless you are listening to both the words **and** the feelings, you are only listening to part of the message.

NON-VERBAL COMMUNICATION

Some experts have calculated that:

- 20% of communication is through words

- 30% of communication is through tone of voice

- 50% of communication is through 'body language'.

If that's correct, 80% of all communication is through non-verbal means.

It takes courage to be open about your feelings, but unless you can say what they are, as well as stating what you think the facts are, you will not be understood.

State your own ideas clearly

If other people talk on two levels, so, of course, do you. Unless you make your own meaning clear, you will also be misinterpreted.

The answer is to find a way of expressing facts and emotions separately, so each can be acknowledged and dealt with. If the facts and feelings get muddled up, it's hard to have a productive conversation.

A phrase such as, "Here's what I think the facts are, and here's what I feel", is simple, direct and allows discussion at both levels.

Acknowledge differences of opinion openly

A good way to visualize what goes on between two people – or two groups of people – is to picture that each one has a 'map of reality'. The map defines what each thinks and believes is true.

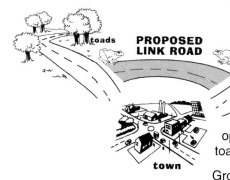

Let's imagine two groups in debate. Group A is responsible for solving a traffic congestion problem in a town. The solution is to build a new link road connecting the two main routes into town, so the traffic can avoid the centre.

The trouble is that the proposed new link road is being opposed by Group B, who point out that a rare species of toad lives there.

Group A can hardly believe the argument. A major improvement that will save money, and probably cut the accident rate, is being held up by 'a bunch of greenies and a few horrible toads'. In turn Group B see their opponents as 'unfeeling bureaucrats with calculators for hearts'.

The problem is that the 'maps of reality' of the two groups have little common ground. Neither group will begin to understand each other until they:

*   Openly express what they feel.

*   State their case clearly **without** using biased and emotional language.

*   Agree to seek an outcome that focuses on the common ground between them.

A simple question that begins to discover that common ground is, "Help me see what you see".

That question acknowledges that there is a difference of opinion – but also acknowledges that the other person's opinion is of importance. In turn, that starts to build some trust and willingness to express true opinions.

Focus on outcomes not personalities

In *Getting to Yes*, Harvard Law Professors Fisher and Ury identified the key skill in any argument. It is the ability to switch away from people's personalities and positions, and on to outcomes or results.

In the town planning example, the two groups had locked further into their individual positions by labelling their opponents in emotional and irrelevant terms.

You begin to achieve a switch from personalities to outcomes when you acknowledge the difference of opinion, and say something like, "What do we need to achieve, so that we would both feel good about the result? How can we achieve it by working together?"

This type of question starts to switch people from defending their existing position, to looking for common ground.

> Separate the personality from the problem!

> *For a co-operative learning group to work effectively, every member needs to feel safe to volunteer opinions and ideas.*
>
> *Few people will feel safe to do so if they feel they will be slapped down or ridiculed.*

Avoid the use of emotional or judgmental phrases

These can be obvious 'put downs' such as 'rubbish', or more subtle criticisms, such as "Few people believe that …".

If an idea is really unworkable, it can be dealt with by saying something like, "Let's consider that suggestion when we've had other ideas put forward." Often the idea just gets dropped naturally.

Other times it is possible to come back to the suggestion and say, "I think there could be problems in the suggestion to … because …". Then list the logical difficulties, without criticizing the person.

At all times maintain the vital distinction between criticizing ideas, and criticizing the person who put forward the idea.

Help others let go of worries

Your group will need to help members talk out any concerns and worries, so they have a clear mind for the task.

One deceptively simple idea is for each member to state – before the group gets down to work – what is on their mind. Many concerns can be laid aside for the duration of the group session, merely by allowing them to surface and by acknowledging them.

> **BUILD POSITIVE ATTITUDES**
>
> Your group will function well when each member appreciates the importance of:
>
> - Being generous with praise for contributions and ideas and showing collaborative skills. And being sparing with criticism!
> - Enthusiasm.
> - Smiling – it takes 72 muscles to frown and just 14 to smile.
> - Looking for why ideas might work, rather than reasons they won't.
> - Humour.
>
>   All these are important ingredients that oil the workings of your group.

M.A.S.T.E.R.
Search out the Meaning

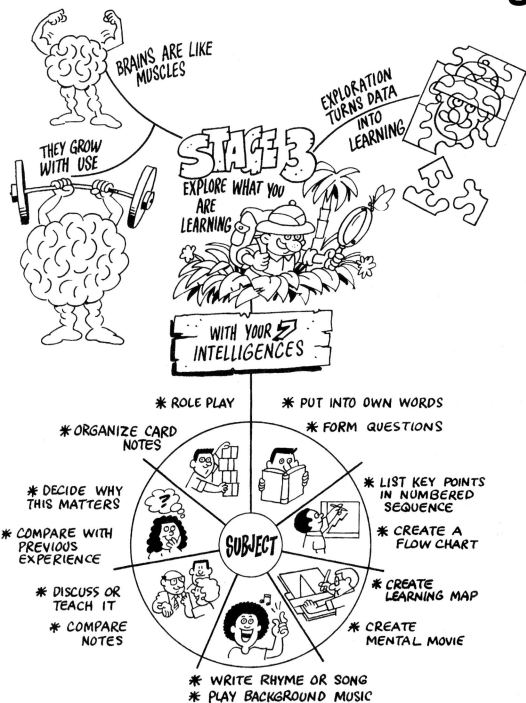

YOUR NOTES

"Active reading is a conversation with the author."
Consequently we invite you to use this page for notes and to ask yourself at least some of these questions.

What was the big idea? What was new?

What assumptions were made? Do I agree with them?

What was fact? Was the evidence reasonable? What was not clear?

What was opinion? Can I accept it? Was any issue oversimplified?

What are my main conclusions? What are the consequences?

How can I use what I've learned?   For my personal learning?   Training?   At home?

What do I want to explore further?

WHAT ELSE MIGHT AFFECT LEARNING STYLES?

WHAT OTHER INTELLIGENCES MIGHT THERE BE?

Stage 4
Trigger the Memory

Short-term v long-term memory

Obviously there can be no learning without memory. So it pays to know a bit about how your memory works, and how to improve it. Especially as 70% of what you learn today can be forgotten in 24 hours if you do not make a special effort to remember it!

You have a short-term memory and a long-term memory. Your short-term memory is designed to hold information temporarily. For example, a phone number you have looked up or a sentence someone said. You remember it just long enough to use it.

You can think of your memory like transferring sheep into a big field. Short-term memory is like a holding pen at the entrance to the field. To transfer the sheep into the field (long-term memory), you need to deliberately drive them in!

Researchers have found that information needs to be repeated or acted on in some way in order to be transferred from your short-term to your long-term memory. Exploring what you have learned, using a range of intelligences, is a way to act on it.

Researchers also note that we have separate memories for sounds, sights and feelings. Which is why it makes sense not just to read something, but repeat it out loud and, if practical, find a way to associate it with a physical movement.

For example, if you are learning a foreign language, you would **read** the word or phrase, **speak** it out loud, and **act** it out in an exaggerated way. [That's the idea behind our Japanese example.]

It also shows why it is important to make notes as you learn from a talk or book. You are then listening and writing. So you involve your memory for **sight** (the notes), **sound** (the talk) and **movement** (the physical action of writing).

SHORT-TERM MEMORY

... is for temporary data.

LONG-TERM MEMORY

... is for important information.

There's nothing wrong with your memory – you just need to use it properly!

BE VERY SELECTIVE!

The trick is to weed out what is really essential to have at your fingertips. Only try to memorize the key points of the subject.

Your memory is already good!

Take a moment and imagine, in your mind's eye, opening your kitchen door. Now, mentally note down **everything** in your kitchen. The cupboards, the kitchen tools, the position of the fridge, oven, microwave, etc, etc. The detail you can remember is incredible. And that's just the kitchen. You could do the same with every other room! Your memory is good – the trick is knowing how to get the best out of it.

You remember most from the beginning and the end of a session

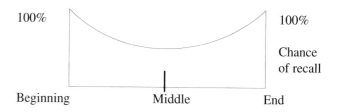

The chart above suggests an important memory strategy. If you want to keep your recall high, have lots of beginnings and endings to your learning session. Most people find it difficult to really concentrate for more than 20 minutes at a time. So don't force yourself into long learning sessions. Stop frequently and take a break.

The effect of taking frequent breaks is to keep your recall level much higher, because you have lots of beginnings and endings!

Level of recall

One long session   A session with three breaks

You normally remember what's unusual

We remember what is odd, bizarre, comical or rude! These things are easy to picture in our minds so they are 'memorable'. If you want to remember something, therefore, try really hard to associate it with a funny, unusual, or even vulgar, mental image. That is exactly what the professional memory men do.

You remember information that is organized

Organizing what you are learning into groups or categories works. The reason is that you are actively doing something with the information, not passively looking at it. You are also forming associations.

Visual memory is the strongest

"A picture", it is said, "is worth a thousand words". It is because of the strength of visual memory that we have emphasized so many visual tools of learning: making a mental picture of what is being learned, making a diagram, chart, sketch, using colour, highlights and underlining. Over 60% of the brain is taken up with visual processing.

When you create your own diagrams or charts, you begin to see the pattern in the information. Suppose you needed to remember the countries in the Far East. Most people have only a hazy idea where they are in relation to each other.

If you were to draw a simplified picture of the various states, however, you would begin to recognize the area. If you went further and drew the map again from memory, and then compared it with your original copy – you'd really begin to 'own' the information.

The four 'R's of memory

In order to recall what you have learned, you need to register it strongly, so it makes an impression. That needs action. The following model, which shows how memory works, helps to define what that action should be.

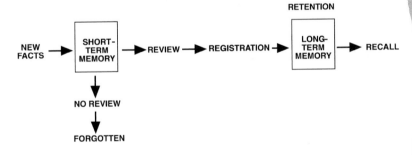

Review – An active attempt to remember.

Registration – Getting it into your long-term memory.

Retention – Keeping it there!

Recall – Getting the facts out when you need them.

The four 'R's' of memory.

If you look at the above model, you will see that if new facts are not reviewed, they simply drop out of the short-term memory. They are forgotten. In one ear and out the other.

If you read about something, repeat it out loud, picture it in your head and jot down a couple of reminder words, you've reviewed it visually, auditorily and physically (the note taking). It is a multi-sensory review.

SUBCONSCIOUS LEARNING

Here's another simple but effective idea for learning foreign languages.

Label the objects around your house with their foreign language names.

You have a constant reminder and an opportunity for subconscious learning.

What is 'review'?

It's an active attempt to register information in your long-term memory. You do so by 'hooking' the facts into your visual, auditory and physical memory. The brain has lots of memory sites, and the more sites (ie: senses) you involve, the better you'll register the new information.

It's like putting reminders up all over your house. The more places to jog your memory, the easier it is to remember.

An ideal time to review what you've learned would be when you go back to the subject after a break. But note that review is **not** the same as simple repetition. Simple repetition, without actively exploring the meaning of the subject, has much less effect.

If you want proof of the value of review look no further than a test done on fifteen-year-olds by researcher Gates. He gave them a list of nonsense syllables to learn. Nonsense words are the most difficult to learn, because they lack meaning.

Here's what he found. Notice the students spent exactly the same length of time on the learning task – it was only the way they spent their time that differed.

% of time reading	% of time spent on review	Average number of syllables remembered
100%	0%	65
80%	20%	92
60%	40%	98
40%	60%	105
20%	80%	137

Time spent reviewing can at least double your recall. Other studies show a four times improvement.

People who do not review as they learn are constantly putting new information in, but then allowing that information to slip away. That makes learning difficult, because there will be less data in their brain on which they can hook – or associate – the next lot of new information.

Spending a little time to register something properly at the beginning, saves a huge amount of time later. The simple truth is that most information is not forgotten, it was never shifted from short-term memory into long-term memory in the first place.

The importance of associations

Think of your memory like a library with thousands of books (ie: facts) stored in it. If the books are stored in a haphazard manner – or in an irrelevant manner such as by size or colour – then it becomes almost impossible to retrieve any one book. There is no logical connection.

However, if the books are stored in an organized way (eg: by subject and author) then retrieval or recall becomes easy and quick. So to remember well, create plenty of strong connections or associations.

Here are two studies that show the value of **active** linking in creating powerful memories.

Study 1

Three groups of students were each asked to learn 10 new words.

Group 1 – just read the words.

Group 2 – sorted the words by type of word.

Group 3 – formed sentences that contained the words.

Result?

Group 3 remembered 250% better than Group 1.

Study 2

The students were asked to learn pairs of words. Like Dove + Car

Group 1 – read the words silently.

Group 2 – read a sentence aloud that contained the words.

Group 3 – made up their own sentence and read it aloud.

Group 4 – made a vivid mental picture where the words interacted with each other, eg: the dove just missed a speeding car.

Which group in Study 2 do you think did the best? Each group did better than the one before it, and the final group learned **three times** better than the first.

How might they improve the results even further?

By asking Group 4 to describe, out loud, their mental image of the words interacting. In this way you would have a story with interactive pictures **and** sound.

"Why," said the dodo, "the best way to explain it is to do it!"

Lewis Carroll
Alice in Wonderland

Sleep on it

Often we 'forget', because the information was never really registered properly. Sometimes, however, information just seems to fade from your memory. For this reason, early researchers thought that memory gradually faded, rather like a curtain can be faded by the sun.

We now know that memory becomes blurred when new information is so similar to what we already know, that the newer experiences simply interfere with our memory of the previous material.

LEARN

REVIEW

SLEEP

REVIEW

Learning is more effective in regular, short bursts of about 30 minutes each.

STRETCHING

Stretching is an effective break. Reach up above your head and pretend to pick grapes from an overhead branch. It gets air into your lungs and your body is refreshed.

You can help combat this process by deliberately interrupting an important learning session by an overnight sleep.

Researcher Chris Evans believes that **the** most important function of sleep is to allow our brain to consider the new things that have been learned during the day. They are then filed and consolidated into our memory system. This happens during Rapid Eye Movement sleep, or R.E.M sleep.

According to this theory, the sleeping brain is like an off-line computer. No new information comes in during sleep, instead the time is taken up with making sense of what we've already experienced or learned.

The implication of this theory is that the ideal pattern would be:

1   **Learn.**   2   **Review the material briefly before sleep.**

3   **Sleep.**   4   **Briefly review the previous day's learning again.**

Researchers have tested this pattern. They asked two groups of students to learn a word list for the same amount of time. Then the first group was tested after eight hours of daytime activity. They scored 9% correct recall. The second group was tested after eight hours sleep. They scored 56% correct recall. Six times higher.

If an intervening sleep isn't practical, a period of different activity, such as listening to music or exercising, will cause less interference and help the process of memory.

The fact that similar material interferes with and therefore weakens memory, would argue for varying your subjects throughout the day.

Memory demands action

There are at least 14 ways to make sure you remember. Here are some tools for remembering both complex information and simpler things such as difficult spellings.

1   **Make a decision to remember**

    The first and most important step you need to take if you are going to commit something to memory is – make a definite decision that you are going to remember.

2   **Take regular breaks**

    After 30 minutes maximum of learning you need to take a break. This break should allow you a complete rest from what you are learning. The break need only be a couple of minutes. Try drinking water at each break – our bodies are more than 70% water and a regular glass of water can keep us more alert.

3 **Use a 'review' cycle**

Repetition is an essential stage in creating long-term memory, so it's important to review what you have learned on a regular basis in the days that follow.

This helps long-term memory to form.

An example of a highly effective review plan is as follows:
a   Learn the material
b   Review it briefly after **an hour**
c   Review it again after **one day**
d   Review it again after **one week**
e   Review it again after **one month**
f   Review it again after **six months**

Each review should take only a very short time – say three to four minutes. And each review should only be of the notes you took or the highlighted sections – never the original book. Only go back to the original book if you want to get clear on something.

This pattern of review can lead to very substantial improvements in remembering. In fact studies have shown that instead of forgetting 70% after 24 hours, you can remember 80% after six months, with this simple sequence of rehearsal.

So, for an expenditure of perhaps 20 - 25 minutes, you could almost triple your ability to memorize.

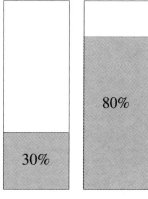

*What you remember after 24 hours **without** a review cycle.*   *What you remember after six months **with** regular short reviews.*

4 **Create multi-sensory memories**

Multi-sensory experiences help us to form long-lasting memories. So, when you want to remember, it will suit you to do everything you can to ensure there is a visual, auditory and physical experience in your learning.

a   **Make notes or a learning map as you learn from a talk.** You listen (Auditory), make the notes or map (Physical) and see what you have written or drawn (Visual)

b   **Remembering the steps in a process**. You watch as someone else demonstrates the process (Visual), say out loud the steps in the process (Auditory), and 'walk through' or act out the steps yourself (Physical), before actually attempting it for real

HOT TIP

Make your own list of the main tools of learning that suit you.

Carry it with you and use it when you are in a training class, lecture or are studying.

5 **Use imagery to remember**

You can strengthen any image by adding movement to it. For example, picture a horse standing – and now galloping. Which is the stronger image? Movement adds memorability.

So if you have a mental image, try moving the image forwards (or backwards) in your mind. Make things dance together or stand on top of one another. You can even add temperature by imaging things as freezing or hot.

Funny things are well remembered, so is the unusual. So use humorous images whenever you can. Detail and movement are the key to a vivid and therefore memorable image.

6   **Try a 'review concert'**

Music helps you relax, and you learn more easily when you are relaxed.

Music also stimulates the emotional part of your brain, where an important element of your long-term memory is situated. And music makes sure your whole brain is involved in the learning. To oversimplify, your right hemisphere works on the music and your left hemisphere deals with the words.

There are certain styles of music that are particularly effective for learning, and we have given you some recommendations in the margin.

You can review what you are learning by simply reading a summary out loud as you listen to the music. Another way to do this is to record a summary of what you want to memorize on an audio cassette and listen to it and your music together.

The aim of playing music while reviewing the material is to create what we call a 'review concert'. You sit back quietly, relax and just listen to the words and music. You will be surprised at how it brings back clear memories of what you have learned – like a 'mental movie'. This is a technique that Accelerated Learning Systems uses successfully in its language learning courses.

7   **'Memory flashing'**

This exotically named way to remember is **extremely** powerful and simple.

a   Take your notes in learning map or brief list form

b   Study them carefully for one or two minutes

c   Then set your notes aside and recreate them from memory

d   Now compare the two learning maps or two sets of notes (ie: the original and the one you just made). You will immediately see anything you missed out

e   Now make a third set of notes or learning map. Again compare your new set of notes or learning map with the original

When the original and your new set of notes are the same, you will have created a very strong memory for your notes – a virtually photographic memory.

Music that is suitable for a review concert includes:

Mozart   *Concerto #21 in C major, K467.*

Beethoven *Piano Concerto #5 in E flat.*

Vivaldi   *Flute Concerto #3 in D major.*

Bach   *Concerto in D minor for two violins.*

Mozart   *Clarinet concerto in A major.*

Pachelbel *'Canon' from Canon and Gigue.*

MEMORY FLASHING

'Memory flashing' is a very powerful way to embed knowledge.

Create the initial learning map

Recreate it from memory

Compare the two. The mind instantly focuses on what was missed.

Try this out for yourself at the end of this book. Prepare a learning map that summarizes the entire book. Then use the memory flashing technique to really store it away permanently. Result? You could remember all the learning and training techniques with one page of notes.

8 Flash cards

Some subjects lend themselves to writing on flash cards. Scientific formulae, for example, or foreign words.

You can make use of spare time – travelling on a train or bus for example – to review the flash cards and test yourself.

9 Flash maps

Flash maps are grown-up versions of flash cards. All you do is create a ring binder for all your learning maps, with dividers in between the subjects. Then file a copy of all your learning maps in this binder.

The great benefit is that you can revise enormous amounts of material during times that would otherwise be wasted.

10 Invent a mnemonic!

A mnemonic (*nem–on–ic*) is just a fancy name for a memory aid.

One of the most useful is an acronym. An acronym is a word made up from the first letters of what you are trying to remember eg: N.A.S.A. – National Aeronautical Space Agency. Or S.C.U.B.A – Self Contained Underwater Breathing Apparatus.

You can compress this type of memory aid into a single word – or a sentence.

M.A.S.T.E.R. is, of course, a mnemonic for the Six Stages of Learning.

11 Let it sink in overnight

If you review your notes on a subject for a few moments before getting ready for bed, your learning will benefit as the brain appears to use sleep as a time to 'file away' new information.

12 Number the points to remember

This simple idea is one of the most useful. If you number the points, ideas or actions you need to remember, then you will automatically know if you have forgotten one!

13 Over-learning

The literature on memory supports the fact that if you really want to remember something you should 'over-learn' it.

"Music begins where words end."

Goethe

Try holding flash cards above eye level. Some people find it helps them memorize better.

OVER-LEARNING

There is good practical proof for 'over-learning'.

Experience tells us that a learning activity like riding a bicycle is never forgotten. We repeat the actions often enough to acquire the skill as a life-long memory.

Memory for physical skills is stored in the part of the brain called the cerebellum.

In other words, for a really crucial piece of information you should not only review it till you 'know it cold' – but even continue to learn it beyond that point. Such information is literally never forgotten because it becomes part of your physical memory. That's why memory flashing works.

14 **Chunk it**

The literature on memory suggests that we can remember up to seven 'bits' of information in our short-term memory. So here is a way of compressing lots of information into an easily recalled format.

a   Make your notes in a learning map form

b   Title each learning map with a single word

c   Invent a seven letter (or less) mnemonic which enables you to remember all the title words

How to match names to faces

The reason why most people find it difficult to remember names is because you hear the name, but see the face, so there is no direct association between the two.

The secret to remembering names is to create a strong visual association between the name and the face. Here's how:

• Start by expecting to remember. Say to yourself, "I **will** remember this person's name".

• Look thoroughly at the newcomer. Concentrate and take in:

The Hair	It's not just hair. It's long or short, straight or curly, black, blond, brown, grey, etc.
The Eyebrows	They are not just strips of hair. They are arched or thin or bushy or meet in the middle.
The Eyes	They are not just brown or blue. They are large or small, close or wide-set.
The Nose	It's small or large, long or snub, narrow or wide, straight or curved.
The Face	It's round or oval or square.

The next step is to create an association between the visual appearance of the face and the name.

• Repeat the person's name straight away – and explain why you are doing so. If it's relevant, ask the person to spell the name for you. People are, naturally, emotionally attached to their name and they will be flattered by your interest.

• If you have time, ask if they know the origin of their name. It's a great way to create a stronger association.

- Look for a visual link between the person's face and their name. Something that associates the physical characteristics of their face with their name. If possible, exaggerate the characteristics like cartoonists do, because that makes them more memorable.

- Ask yourself "Who else do I know with the same name?", and try to picture the two people interacting in some way. (You don't ever have to say what you thought of!)

- Finally, visualize the person's name stamped on their forehead!

When you say goodbye, repeat the name again, and make a decision to recall the place where you first met.

In summary, the skill is to:

a   Really concentrate hard on the face

b   Find a way to link the sound of the name with the appearance of face

The real reason we forget names is because we hardly ever try to remember them. We glance at the person, hear the name IN OUR SHORT-TERM MEMORY, but make no effort to actually move it over to our long-term memory. It is not that we forget the name – it just never entered our long-term memory at all.

*When you really **look**, rather than glance at a face, you will see an incredible variation in detail. You have now registered the face strongly.*

SUCCESS = EFFORT

Many people are disappointed with this formula for remembering names. They expected a 'party trick'. A magic idea that takes one minute to learn, and requires no effort to do.

Unfortunately, memory (and learning) aren't like that. The 'secret' of success is very simple. Learn the skill and make an effort to apply it.

Remembering numbers

Here's a good way to remember your passport or P.I.N. number instantly and forever.

Say your number is 4285. Simply invent a memorable phrase or sentence that uses a four letter, two letter, eight letter and five letter word. Memorize the phrase and you can always work out the number. Words are easier to remember than numbers because they mean something!

A phrase might be 'grab my invested money'.
　　　　　　　　　　 4　　 2　　　8　　　　　5

Of course you can use the idea for dates, birthdays, formulae, passports, social security numbers and anything numerical, eg:

186,282 miles per second. The speed of light.

How about … 'A dazzling sunray is flashing by'?
　　　　　 1　　 8　　　 6　　2　　8　　　2

Remembering what you've forgotten

When we forget something, we tend to concentrate on what it is that we have forgotten. But that's illogical reasoning, because we **have** forgotten it!

A REMINDER

Want to be sure to remember something important later in the day?

Switch your watch to your other hand. It's a constant reminder that something is different.

WHERE WAS I?

WHAT WAS I THINKING?

WHAT DID I SAY?

WHO WAS THERE?

WHAT LETTER DOES IT BEGIN WITH?

ANSWER

Instead use the power of association. Retrace in your mind what led up to, and what followed, the forgotten event, name, fact, or article. What were you doing, thinking, feeling, saying? Who were you with? What were your physical surroundings?

Think of it like a hole into which the forgotten item has disappeared. You are interested in examining only the surroundings of that hole in great detail. When you have all the associations, say to yourself **positively,** "I shall shortly remember". And then leave it to your subconscious. You will usually find that the answer will emerge.

Sometimes it's a help to add another association by slowly going through the alphabet. In most cases you will get a strong feeling for which letter of the alphabet the forgotten item begins with. That triggers the memory.

TRAINING TIPS

Helping the group memorize the subject

This can be a short and simple element of the training day.

Again, work out for yourself what is likely to be effective from the learning techniques we have discussed. Some ideas that have worked well for us include:

- Getting teams to create **a mnemonic** to summarize the day – and compete for the best. Or create a memory map of the day.

- Invite the whole group to close their eyes and listen to a **concert review** – a quietly spoken summary of the day that you will have pre-prepared. What's different is that you will be reading it over a background of classical music. Page 90 gives some suitable examples.

The theory is that the summary allows the group to replay the highlights of the day in their minds. It becomes memorable due to the unusual nature of the activity, the fact that the music and words activate different halves of the brain and because the music directly accesses the limbic system, or middle brain, where much of your memory processes seem to be.

Certainly most trainees comment afterwards that they remember this session vividly the next day.

REVIEW HELPS MEMORY

To really become expert at anything requires practice. Knowing something once does not guarantee you'll know it for ever.

Just as sportsmen need constant practice, so you need to keep your learning topped up regularly.

PARENT TIPS

Memory strategies for students

All of these ideas are invaluable to help your child. In fact, I have personal experience that the simple strategy of memory flashing alone can have a major impact on a student's performance. As can the use of flash cards, numbering key points, mnemonics and the review pattern on pages 90 – 91.

Improve your child's spelling – instantly!

To remember the spelling of a particular word, simply create a multi-sensory image of that word to establish it in your long-term memory.

1   First 'chunk' the word down into syllables. For example, the word 'psychiatrist' would be split up as ...
    PSY – CHI – A – TRIST.

    First pronounce the individual letters in the first syllable, ie: P-S-Y. Then say the whole syllable, ie: 'SY'.

    Next spell out the second syllable, ie: C-H-I. Then pronounce the second syllable, ie: 'KI'. Next the third syllable, ie: 'A'.

    Finally spell out the fourth T-R-I-S-T, and then pronounce it, ie: 'TRIST'.

2   Now visualize the syllables as if they were written on a blackboard in white chalk. Imagine the blackboard is slightly above your eye level. Close your eyes and repeat the individual letters and then the sound of the syllables. Try to see the letters clearly.

3   Now create another strong visual memory by writing the word out in bold letters OR write over the word several times in different colours OR write a word in a way that suggests its meaning, eg:
    S – E – P – A – R – A – T – E.

4   Complete the auditory memory by saying and spelling the word out loud as a complete word.

This is an important strategy to teach to children.

The most commonly mis-spelled words in offices are:

practice (noun) / practise (verb)
withhold
occurred
benefited
principal (most important)
principle (guiding idea)
incur
grievance
concede
competent
calendar
acquire
accommodation

Try out the method opposite for any words that may have given you trouble!

CORRECT MIS-SPELLING
Keep a list of the words you misspell most frequently. Emphasize where you used to make a mistake with capitals, eg:

Wrong	**Right**
seperate	*sepArate*
changable	*changEable*
privelege	*privIlege*
independant	*independEnt*
analize	*analYze*
rythm	*rHythm*
grammer	*grammAr*

M.A.S.T.E.R.
Trigger the Memory

YOUR NOTES

"Active reading is a conversation with the author."
Consequently we invite you to use this page for notes and to ask yourself at least some of these questions.

What was the big idea? What was new?

What assumptions were made? Do I agree with them?

What was fact? Was the evidence reasonable? What was not clear?

What was opinion? Can I accept it? Was any issue oversimplified?

What are my main conclusions? What are the consequences?

How can I use what I've learned?   For my personal learning?   Training?   At home?

What do I want to explore further?

Stage 5
Exhibit What you Know

You now have the right **M**ind Set – relaxed, confident and ready for learning (Stage 1). You've **A**cquired the facts in ways that suit you (Stage 2). You've **S**earched out the meaning using a range of your intelligences, and have therefore understood it properly (Stage 3). You've made a deliberate effort to **T**rigger your memory for what you've learned (Stage 4).

You now need a short session to demonstrate to yourself that you really have understood the subject, and that you can put it into practice. You must 'show you know'.

Test yourself

This is where the learning tools you have already assembled can come into their own. If it's information you are learning, try going over your memory maps or notes. Try memory flashing!

Test yourself with flash cards. Create a 'mental movie' of what you have learned. Do you remember it all? Recreate a flow chart. Try teaching or explaining it to someone else. Create a logical, numbered list. Repeat it out loud in your own words. Learning tools can be used for exploring, memorizing **and** testing your learning.

When you make testing yourself an automatic part of the process of learning, you can become more matter-of-fact about mistakes. Errors become helpful feedback about how you are progressing, clarifying any areas of doubt or inability. So an error that you learn from is a sign of progress.

OPPORTUNITY NOT THREAT

A test is a chance to explore the limits of what you can currently do or understand. It's an opportunity not a threat.

"Mistakes are just staging posts on the road to success."

Learning a language

Flash cards are an excellent way to test yourself.

Write the English word on one side of the card and use the other side for the language you are learning.

Learning a process

Test yourself by drawing a flow-chart of the proper sequence. Also redraw the important diagrams you have studied in a manual.

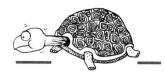

"The turtle only makes progress when his neck is stuck out."

Rollo May

Mistakes represent a chance to see what needs more attention. So concentrate, not on **how many** mistakes you may have made, but on **what type** of mistakes they are.

For example, an accounting student who initially felt depressed at 29 mistakes out of 100 attempts came to realize that he was really making the same type of mistake over and over again. He corrected the misunderstanding that led to the errors, and started producing fault-free work.

Practise what you've learned

Use **mental rehearsal** to see yourself actually using what you have learned. It is a method used with great success by top class sportsmen.

Use **role play** to act out what you have learned alone or with someone else. Role play gives you a further chance to improve or refine your skills without risk and before you use them for real. Again, it is a good confidence builder.

Learning a language

Imagine a situation in which you want to be able to use the language you are learning. Practise the conversation you would have – aloud – using appropriate gestures and body language.

Learning a process

Use your imagination and go through an important sequence step-by-step. Make the detail really vivid in your mental rehearsal.

"Every job is a self-portrait of the person who did it."

One of the things that happens with 'formal' learning is that we get used to other people judging us – marking our work. However, it's obviously more satisfying when we become the quality judges of our own work.

That's why the stage of 'show you know' is so important. You set your own standards and you check your own performance against them.

Use it!

If an idea is used within 24 hours of seeing or hearing about it, research shows it is much more likely to be used permanently. So, if you want what you have learned to stick, use it straight away.

Watch other people and take careful note of how they use the same skills that you are learning. Research also shows that when you learn from more than one person, you are more able to use the skill in different situations.

"Practice doesn't make perfect.

Perfect practice makes perfect!"

Vince Lombardi
American football coach

It's not automatic to remember to use a new skill. So put up some reminders to yourself. A simple note stuck on a fridge or notice board. A hand-out from a training session stuck in a prominent place. Or make yourself a book mark with the learning strategies on it that work best for you.

Learn with your family

Make a real attempt to involve your family in your learning. If you let them help – for example, by asking them to listen while you explain what you have learned – they are also likely to gain from it.

A family that is involved and understands what it is you are trying to achieve is less likely to feel resentment about the time you need to devote to learning.

Study buddies

Find yourself a learning partner – somebody who is also learning what you are learning. You can offer each other support as you explore the subject and you can regularly quiz each other to check how you are doing.

Study buddies help by testing each other and by comparing their different approaches.

Mentors

Find yourself a mentor – someone who is highly skilled in the area you are learning about, and who would be encouraging, supportive and a source of further information for you.

A mentor should be somebody with whom you can feel comfortable and who can offer positive feedback, constructive criticism and ideas to try. **You can also learn from his or her mistakes!**

It's a pity that we normally grow up regarding advice as something that always comes 'from the top downwards'. We rarely ask for it, it's normally imposed on us.

If you fail to seek advice from the people around you, you are cutting yourself off from a major source of information, and self-advancement.

Here's some advice about advice!

- Ask for it frequently – people like to give it. It's flattering.

- Keep an open mind. Experts are good at giving accurate factual information. Many are less good at giving judgements.

- Avoid being defensive. Someone can criticize your actions and work without criticizing you personally. Make the distinction between the two!

INSTINCTIVE COMPETENCE

To start with, you have to think about riding a bike.

You have to concentrate on what you are doing – it feels awkward – and you fall off a lot!

Gradually, as you practise, it becomes an unconscious skill.

You no longer need to think about it. You just do it instinctively.

Practice is the only route to instinctive competence.

TRAINING TIPS

Helping them exhibit what they know

This can be a highlight of the training day. By now the learning should have been complete. What they need now is a way to 'Show they Know'.

Almost any TV game show can be adopted with success.
For example, you can create a $64,000 question game.
Or a quiz based on any board game involving a race – correct answers win points and moves. You can even get the trainees to think up the questions.

One of the very best games is a game we call 'Swap Shop'. It's simple but is a good example of a multi-intelligence game.

Give each member three post cards. First ask them, as individuals, to write the three most actionable ideas from the day on three separate cards.

Next ask them to get up and swap one of these cards with some one else.

When they have done that, ask them to get into groups of five and agree on the three best ideas from the 15 they have.

Finally, have each group report to the whole room.

This activity is structured so that each learner eventually sees all the best good ideas from the day – their own and other people's.

MISTAKES

The person who does not make mistakes, does not make anything!

Too often we feel that errors reflect on us as individuals, and they affect our self-esteem.

That's wrong. An error should be seen as quite separate from the person who makes it.

> "They know enough who know how to learn."
>
> **Henry Adams**
> *The Education of Henry Adams*

PARENT TIPS

How to exhibit what she knows

There are good ideas here for students, eg: study buddies, flash cards and mentors.

Tests

Your children are going to be exposed to tests throughout their academic life. So it's important that they see these tests as helpful rather than threatening.

That's why you should explain that errors are actually helpful indications of what needs attention. What **type** of mistake is it? Does it indicate that something is not yet understood or was it an error of carelessness? If so, was it because the question was not properly read before he rushed in with an answer? (Which is the most common reason!)

Grade your own work

One of the most important mind shifts a student needs to make is this. She is working, not for the teacher, but for herself. Make that shift and you have a more motivated student and one who becomes more committed to the quality of her own work.

Encourage her to grade her own work before she hands it in. Is it up to her own best standard? When she gets it back, encourage her to ask her teacher what she could have done to have got an even better grade. That way the teacher is working for her – not vice-versa!

Learning logs

Schools now operate Records of Achievement – files of typical work that the pupil has produced and that the pupil retains throughout school life.

You can add to this with a simple learning log. Brief details noted in a book each week of new concepts grasped. It can also be where he records areas – or even individual words – that are proving difficult to understand. Can you find out together? He is controlling his own learning and not passively waiting to be taught.

PRACTICAL PRACTICE

Write out the learning strategies you intend to use. One each on a card. Then lay out each card in a separate place where you work or study.

Or in a diary, one per day.

Or pin them to the wall.

Or carry them with you.

Practise each technique one at a time until it becomes a habit.

SEPARATE THE ACTION FROM THE CHILD

For a parent to say, "Bad boy" confuses the person with the deed.

If you disagree with a child on an issue, address the issue rather than criticizing them as a person.

Rather than, "You are a bad boy for leaving your room untidy", a more appropriate response might be, "I love you and the state of your room at the moment is not what I would expect of you".

SUPER SKILL 5

Mark Twain, as usual, put it well, "If we taught our children to speak in the way that we teach them to write – everyone would stutter".

By this he meant that, because we expect our writing to be perfect straight away, we are unable to write with fluency and ease.

Power writing

Very often we need to show we've learned something in a report, speech, or inter-company memo. So some principles of clear writing constitute a Super Skill.

To write well you have to concentrate first on 'what', then on 'how'. Content comes before style.

The problem is that most people expect to write creatively **and** edit what they are writing, both at the same time. The result is that writing becomes stressful and stilted.

The secret is to write quickly and fluently, and then, **after** you have finished this first speedy draft, allow yourself to criticize and edit your writing. Computers today make the process easy.

Creative mapping

Assume that you have a subject on which you need to write. Try this sequence:

1   Go to any previous notes or reference books you need.

2   Put the subject of your article in the middle of a blank page.

3   Now allow your mind the luxury of free association.

> **QUANTITY LEADS TO QUALITY**
>
> The best guarantee of having good ideas is to have lots of them!
>
> This 'free flow' stage is called 'brainstorming'. Put down all the ideas, even apparently silly ones.
>
> This is because 'irrelevant' ideas can often be stepping stones to truly creative ideas.

Just write down on the page all the ideas and words that come to mind. Let the ideas branch out as they form in your head.

Do this for 15 minutes. It is vital to keep going – even after you seem to have run out of ideas. This is because your first ideas will be the most obvious ones. If you stop too early, you will only have captured the more mundane thoughts.

The whole point is to keep the logical, critical editor in you at bay!

4   Sit back and look at your map.

5   Now start a new creative map, this time grouping related ideas together in bigger clusters. Each bigger cluster will be a theme you will develop.

"The purpose of education is to replace an empty mind with an open one."

Malcolm Forbes

I have given an example here of how I 'mapped out' this session on power writing with a creative outline.

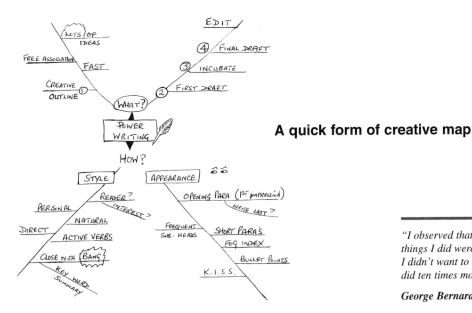

A quick form of creative map

> "I observed that nine out of ten things I did were failures. I didn't want to be a failure so I did ten times more work."
>
> **George Bernard Shaw**

Free flow writing

Now, with the organized 'map' of your subject in front of you, start to write your report, communication or speech.

Again, just write. Don't worry yet about style, spelling, grammar or punctuation. Allow your now organized thoughts to flow down on the paper. Write up one cluster, then move on to the next. Keep going as quickly as you can until you finish.

Do nothing!

Good writing involves about 40% research, 20% writing and 40% revision.

No-one has ever written anything of value without at least one re-write. If it is going to be good – expect several re-writes. The whole point of your free flow writing session was to make it spontaneous. That means it won't be perfect. But it won't be stilted either!

You now need a period where you switch off thinking about the subject consciously. A period of incubation. During this fallow time, your subconscious mind will probably be filling in missing sections and remembering extra points. It may also be working on better ways of expressing what you meant. It is another example of the power of reflection.

EG:

Make sure you include examples of what you are writing about.

Examples bring your writing to life.

Edit

After a break – overnight if possible – you can return to your report or writing.

Now is the time to be conscious about style. Now is the time to be critical.

Early in the morning is often an excellent time to start editing. The day has not yet crowded out the potential contributions from your subconscious mind. Approach the edit session as if you were reading your words with a stranger's eyes.

Is the meaning clear? Is there a flow to the writing? Do you 'tell them what you are going to tell them, tell them, and then tell them what you've told them?'

In other words, do you set up your basic argument or point, then prove it, then conclude with a short summary? A big picture, detail, then a review! That's a satisfying shape for most subjects.

The words, too, should be satisfying. It helps to read out loud what you have written. The aim is that the reader should feel you are communicating directly to him or her.

Good writing mostly has a conversational tone to it. Of course, for some subjects a rather more formal style may be appropriate – but don't confuse sounding serious with being stuffy.

Style

You only have one chance to make a first impression so be natural, be personal, be brief and grab them in the first line.

Your opening paragraph sets the tone. Consider writing or re-writing it after your whole essay or report is finished.

Rule 1 **Consider your audience**

Who are they? What do they expect? What are they interested in? When you answer that question, you begin to define the style, shape and length of your article, report or speech.

Rule 2 **Grab them by the throat!**

Most people do not want to read what you have written!

They will give you the benefit of the doubt during the first paragraph. Therefore you have about 30 seconds to lure them **willingly** into your report or speech. So make the first few words count.

What goes for business correspondence also goes for school, college or training papers. Here are two sales letters that illustrate the point.

CLUTTER

The average person sees hundreds of advertising messages a day. In addition, they read thousands of words of a newspaper and hear thousands more words from the radio news. That doesn't count words from entertainment media, like novels or TV.

All this bombardment is what advertising copywriters call 'clutter'. If your writing is to have any chance of grabbing your readers' attention, it must stand out from this clutter.

READ ON …

These opening sentences make you want to read on.

"Shakespeare was as much a psychologist as an author."

"Your brain can make more connections than all the telephone extensions in the world!"

"Right now, you are worth $3 million. That's a conservative estimate of what a college graduate will earn over his or her career span."

"This company could double its profits through five simple changes."

Dear Sir/Madam

Our new product range

Further to our recent telephone conversation with your good selves, we have pleasure in enclosing our brochure describing our exciting range of self-tapping, bronze-plated widgets. They incorporate the latest anti-rust coatings…"
Etc, etc.

Dear Ms Cartwright

Rust costs your company a lot of money each year. And it causes accidents.

You can save money right **now**, by using our bronze-plated widgets.

They cost no more, and they are self-tapping too.

The first letter is a turn-off, impersonal and cold. The second letter above sets up a problem that the receiver cares about – then solves it. It is directed at the reader in natural, **personal** language. It grabs attention.

Rule 3 **Give them a reason to be interested**

The reader will always want to know, **"What will it do for me?"** You do not write for yourself – you write for the reader.

They don't care about your new product! The only thing they care about is what it might do for them. So start with a benefit. This is not just true of sales letters, it is true of all letters.

Rule 4 **Talk to the reader in active language**

The four characteristics of good writing are:

1 Be clear

2 Be simple

3 Be sincere

4 Be logical

"Important advances have been made in brain research over the last decade. Universities as far apart as Harvard, Yale and UCLA in the United States, and London and Oxford in the UK, are reporting that intelligence is more complex than had been thought, and that it can be increased by the careful application of new ways of teaching and training."

"You can increase your intelligence.

Intelligence is largely a set of skills that can be learned and practised.

This is the conclusion from 10 years of intensive research at leading American and British Universities."

The first example is impersonal, uses the passive tense, and is wordy.

The second example addresses you with news of value and uses **active** language.

'The fielder was hit by the ball' is passive. 'The ball hit the fielder' is more direct, vivid and active. Active language engages your senses.

OPEN WITH A BANG

Will your opening remarks on your next communication make the reader want to find out more?

John Keats, the poet, originally wrote, "Something beautiful is forever a joy".

The line hardly rings too many bells, does it?

"A thing of beauty is a joy for ever."

Now there's a sentence!

Rule 5 **Keep it short**

People respond best to short sentences. With a long sentence, it is all too easy to forget what was said at the beginning! So you lose track and get bored or irritated.

A general rule for editing is that you can tighten up the original draft by one third to one half. The Ten Commandments take up just 297 words. The Gettysburg address required 287 words. People remember punchy sentences.

It's at the revision stage – after a period of incubation – that most of the great lines of history are crafted.

John Kennedy, "Ask not what your country can do for you; ask what you can do for your country".

Martin Luther King, "I have a dream".

The Fog Index

There is a very effective 'measurement' invented by Robert Gunning of The Robert Gunning Clear Writing Institute of Santa Barbara, California. It was developed for journalists writing in English. But the principles are true in any language.

SERIOUS ISN'T DULL

It's true that much business and academic writing is expected to look 'serious'. Serious does not mean dull, however.

It is called the 'Fog Index', and it aims to measure the reading level of a piece of writing.

You take a sample piece of writing about 150 words long. Then calculate the average number of words per sentence.

Next count the number of words that contain three syllables or more. Express this as a percentage of the total number of words. Add the two figures together and divide by 2.5.

So if the average number of words per sentence was   12

And the percentage of words with three syllables or more was 18

The Fog Index would be $12 + 18 \div 2.5 =$ 12

Time Magazine and the Wall Street Journal average 11. The Readers' Digest averages 10.

If you want to reach people, even in business reports, beware of a Fog Index over 12 – unless the subject is very technical. Research shows that 50% of readers get lost if a sentence exceeds 14 words. 80% get lost if it exceeds 20 words!

Some word processing programmes even have a built-in Fog Index.

Generally you are safe with sentences that average 10-14 words.

Use concrete words rather than abstract words. That makes it easier for your reader to visualize what you have written. Apply the Fog Index to your own writing and tailor it to match your readership.

Rule 6 **Make it look inviting**

Whatever you think of the content of this book, it is broken up into reasonably short paragraphs. It **looks** readable.

If you want to emphasize something special, you can even indent an entire paragraph. Just as we have this one.

The result is that the whole section looks more inviting and you have emphasized a key point.

If you look at this book – you will see other ways we have tried to keep you involved.

- We used quotes. I keep my own 'learning log' and, when I see a really good quote, I write it down. A good quote is punchy, relevant and has a ring to it.

- We used bullet points.

- We broke up passages with headings and sub-headings. This is perhaps the most important of all the ways of making your writing user-friendly. They work because they provide a continuous big picture.

- We used metaphors and, wherever possible, painted pictures with words.

Introducing a passage with a phrase like 'Picture this', invites your reader to participate in what you have written.

Wherever possible start with examples to illustrate your point – or even actual drawn illustrations themselves. Most people learn best when they go from the concrete to the abstract. In other words, do it first, analyze it afterwards!

Rule 7 **Close with a bang!**

You have opened with an attention grabber. You have deliberately used basic words, shortish sentences and active verbs.

You have, above all, written to interest the reader. You have written as if it were a personal communication from you to them.

All you need now is a punchy close.

That often can be a relevant quote and a sentence, or at most a short paragraph, that summarizes the theme of what you have said.

So go back over your 'piece' – as journalists call it – and highlight the absolutely key words. Ten to 25 words at most. Now find the shortest way of linking them together. That's your close. It provides the final 'review' for the reader.

K.I.S.S

K.I.S.S. stands for Keep It Short & Simple.

The test of good writing is how pleasurable it is to read. Always choose the simplest, most familiar word that conveys your meaning accurately. Avoid 'lawyer's language'.

Avoid	*Use*
Expeditious	*quick*
Ascertain	*find out*
In the event of	*if*
Commence	*start*
In the majority of cases	*most*
Endeavour	*try*
Due to the fact that	*because*
Assuring you of our best attention	*We appreciate your business*

ACTION

Take a piece of writing that you have produced in the last few months and consider it against the above advice:

1 *Was it appropriate for your audience? Did you visualize the person who would be reading it? Did you write it with him/her in mind, giving them a reason to be interested?*

2 *Did you grab their attention in the opening paragraph? Did the opening one or two paragraphs set out your basic theme?*

3 *Was the language active and direct?*

4 *Were the sentences reasonably short and clear?*

5 *Did you use the simplest words that were appropriate for the readership?*

6 *Did it look inviting?*

7 *Did it close with a 'bang'?*

M.A.S.T.E.R.
Exhibit What you Know

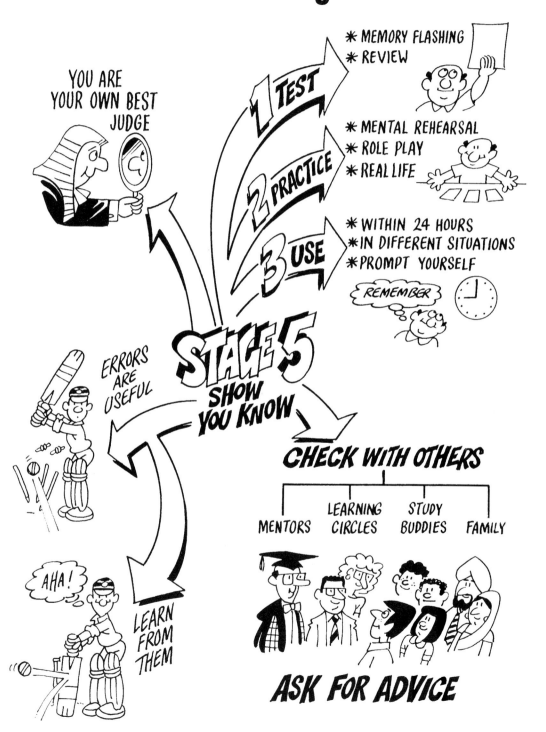

YOUR NOTES

"Active reading is a conversation with the author."
Consequently we invite you to use this page for notes and to ask yourself at least some of these questions.

What was the big idea? What was new?

What assumptions were made? Do I agree with them?

What was fact? Was the evidence reasonable? What was not clear?

What was opinion? Can I accept it? Was any issue oversimplified?

What are my main conclusions? What are the consequences?

How can I use what I've learned?   For my personal learning?   Training?   At home?

What do I want to explore further?

Stage 6
Reflect on <u>How</u> you Learned

Self-assessment

Reflecting on how you've done something is an important element in building any skill – not just learning.

Two simple but powerful questions to ask are:

What went well?   **What could have gone better?**

Keep asking those questions and you've learned the essence of self-assessment.

Use the PERSONAL PROGRESS PLAN that follows to reflect on what you have learned through this book. Notice it can be used, not just to reflect on this particular book, but to reflect on **anything** in your life.

"Plans are only good intentions unless they immediately degenerate into hard work."

Peter Drucker

```
┌──────── A PERSONAL PROGRESS PLAN ════════┐

   •  The most important things I learned are:

   •  As a result I will do this/use the following ideas:

   •  I can expect this initial difficulty – but I will
      overcome it by the following action:

   •  I will check on my own progress. I will know
      I have succeeded when:

   •  I will reward my own success by:

   •  I need to learn more about this:

   •  I will ask this/these person/s to help:

└──────────────────────────────────────────┘
```

"You cannot teach a man anything. You can only help him discover it within himself."

Galileo

"In order to succeed, double your failure rate."

Thomas Watson
Founder of IBM

EGGZACTLY!

Only one creature ever sat down to succeed. A chicken!

"A man grows tired by standing still."

Chinese proverb

The personal progress plan

- It's realistic about the likelihood of difficulties as you actually use what you have learned. If you prepare for a difficulty you will not be easily put off when you meet it.

  Stumbling blocks can be expected when you try something new. See them as helpful feedback. You turn stumbling blocks into stepping stones when you ask the question: "What can I learn from this, to do better next time?"

- It allows for self-assessment. You decide what you regard as success – "I will know I have succeeded when ...". You can work out your own standards by asking yourself "What could I do if I was really competent at this?" That's the standard to aim for.

- It allows for rewards for success – 'Catching yourself doing it right'. Recognize and reward yourself for each success along the way and learning becomes a pleasurable habit.

Author Stephen Covey suggests there are several characteristics of highly successful people. We suggest that three characteristics stand out above all others.

1   They have a clear vision of what success will be like.

START WITH THE END IN MIND

That vision brings with it commitment, determination and a plan.

2   They take personal responsibility for all their actions.

One of the fundamental truths to meet the challenges of life is this. You may not choose what happens to you – but you **always** have a choice of how you react. This is the essence of free will.

IF IT'S TO BE – IT'S UP TO ME

You can choose to be calm or to be angry. You can choose kindness over being hurtful. You can choose to be active or passive. You can choose to seek your maximum potential or you can choose to 'coast along' without extending yourself.

3   They continuously reflect on what they have done.

LEARN FROM YOUR MISTAKES

Then they draw lessons for the future.

Pushing your comfort zone

One of the main messages from this book is that people learn well and easily when they **start** by using learning strategies that match their learning styles.

However, if someone were to finish this book and label himself or herself as 'just a visual learner' or a person who 'can only learn well if they can use their physical and inter-personal intelligence', we will have failed.

When we put labels on ourselves, we start to restrict ourselves. We cut ourselves off from new ideas, new methods and new subjects because they don't fit into our image of what we **think** we can do.

It takes courage to move from your comfort zone – but the rewards can be dazzling!

The techniques that initially seem the least comfortable may be the very tools you need to use to ensure that you overcome potential 'blind spots'.

Success really comes when you move to the edge of your comfort zone and attempt something new and challenging. Meeting and overcoming challenges is what personal development is about.

Some of our happiest moments are when we stretch ourselves to reach new heights and develop new skills. Which would you enjoy more? To play a game you win easily, or to play a game you have to stretch every nerve to win?

GO FOR IT!

In the final analysis, all great achievements have been accomplished by people acting on the conviction of their own vision.

Have you ever seen a park statue dedicated to a committee?

If you become aware of your preferences and strengths and use them, you'll find learning is easier and faster. If you push to the edge of your comfort zone and build a wide range of learning techniques, if you use the **whole** range of your intelligences, then you will have equipped yourself for lifelong learning and success.

"Good administration without vision is like straightening the deck chairs on the Titanic."

You will have truly become an Accelerated Learner!

"It's when you reach out and stretch yourself that you grow as a person."

TRAINING TIPS

Helping them reflect on how they learned

"Every day is a new life to a wise man!"

Bertrand Russell

The last stage of reflection, rather like the first stage of creating a respective state of mind, receives less attention from trainers than it should.

Yet research from American psychologist Kurt Lewin shows that, when learners are able to discuss what they have learned, they are **10 times** more likely to change their future behaviour than when they are merely given information, without the opportunity for reflection.

This can be as simple as writing two headings on a flip chart:

'WHAT COULD HAVE GONE BETTER?'   'WHAT WENT WELL?'

The answers give you, as the trainer, an immediate feedback on the training day.

This is also where you will revert to the opening flip chart where you asked for the learners' expectations and concerns to see how well the session met their expectations and eliminated their concerns.

You might finally ask the trainees to fill out their personal progress plans. The whole point of training is to turn knowledge into action.

PARENT TIPS

Learning from experience

Children are not naturally reflective! But the ability to learn from mistakes, make plans and allocate time sensibly is critical to their success.

So when your child produces a piece of work of lower quality than normal, ask her what she's learned from that. Remind her: **"It's only a mistake if you don't learn from it."**

Similarly emphasize that we all have setbacks, but we can always choose how we react. You can be a victim and feel crushed or you can positively look for a solution.

Your child learns his most important lessons, not from school, but from you: his attitude, his determination and his values.

Think of your true potential like a combination lock.

It is the unique combination of how you like to use your senses and eight intelligences that accounts for your own natural and individual approach to learning.

HOW COMMITTED ARE YOU?

The Spanish explorer, Cortez, had a novel form of motivation for his men. When he landed on the shore of Mexico he set fire to his own ships and presented them with the choice "Win or die!". Thus was born the phrase: 'Burning your boats behind you'.

Success has a lot to do with determination and persistence.

M.A.S.T.E.R.

A Learning Map of What You've Learned

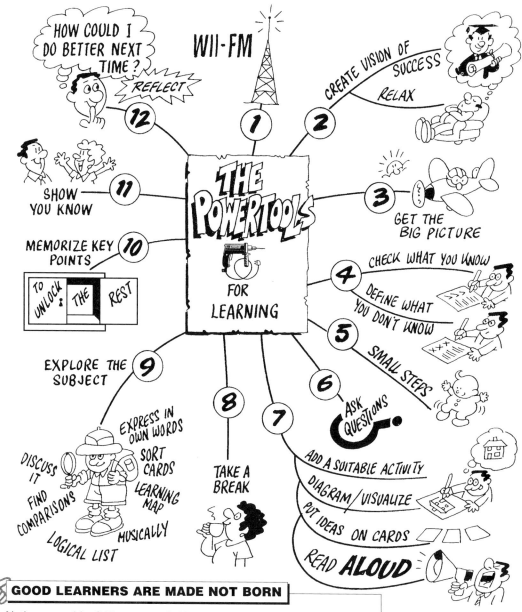

GOOD LEARNERS ARE MADE NOT BORN

Notice something? These are all things you can learn **how** to do.

In other words, good learners are made, not born. Success doesn't depend on past performance – anyone can become an effective learner.

A checklist of learning tools

Tick the techniques you intend to use

M

Decide WII-FM ☐ Create a vision of success ☐ Write down your goals ☐ Create an action plan ☐
Plan your time ☐ Create a positive study environment ☐ Replay an image of past success ☐
Use affirmations ☐ **Relax**! ☐ Take frequent breaks ☐

A

Check the contents page/Sub-heads/Illustrations/Opening paragraphs ☐

Make a preliminary learning map ☐ Other form of notes ☐ Define what you **don't** know ☐

Turn every heading into a question ☐ Ask what does this **mean**? Do I agree? What can I conclude? ☐
Interrogate the author ☐ eg, Does this make sense? What's the evidence for this?

V.
A.
P.

Highlight in colour ☐ Diagram ☐ Learning map ☐ Visualize it ☐ Make a poster ☐
Read aloud dramatically ☐ Make an audio tape ☐ Explain it to someone else ☐
Write and circle key points ☐ Make notes on post cards ☐ Make a model/Learning map ☐

S
E X P L O R E

Discuss/Teach it to someone else. Compare notes ☐

Create a learning map or poster. Visualize it as a TV documentary ☐

Act it out/Role play/Model it/ Use post cards to order your thoughts ☐

List main points in logical order. Analyze it (A.E.I.O.U.) Create a flow chart ☐

Consider how this relates to what you already know and why it matters to you ☐

Summarize it in your own words ☐

Write a jingle, song or rap. Play background (classical) music as you learn ☐

T

Create an inter-active image ☐ Create a mnemonic ☐ Memory flash it ☐
Do a review concert ☐ Review the material on a **regular** basis ☐

E

Test yourself through learning maps or flash cards ☐

Practise through role play or mental rehearsal ☐

Keep a learning log ☐

R

Use a personal progress plan ☐

Push your comfort zone sometimes ☐

Create a learning action circle ☐

BECOMING A LEARNING ORGANIZATION

Everybody benefits when an organization becomes a learning organization – defined as a company that is able continuously to learn and adapt to take advantage of new opportunities and avoid threats.

The speed of change and complexity of modern business is such that companies simply won't survive unless they do become learning organizations. Jack Welch, the Chief Executive Officer of the giant General Electric Company, puts it exactly right: "If the rate of change outside of you is greater than the rate of change inside you – the end is nigh!"

It happened to the dinosaurs, of course. And it's happened to hundreds of thousands of dinosaur companies who simply didn't foresee changes and trends in their markets and react fast enough.

What's new about a learning organization is the realization that today companies can't be run by one 'super brain' at the top. Instead, everyone must be crystal clear about the company's aims so that they can take responsibility to learn the skills and knowledge that we need to achieve those aims.

We need, as we said at the beginning, to 'mobilize every ounce of intelligence in our organization'.

But a learning organization must also actively support its staff to help them achieve their own personal ambitions. And it must look for ways to support their children's learning. So it's a two-way process. You help us learn, we help you and your family learn. This book is a first step.

NOTE

This section needs to be read from the perspective of an employee working within an organization which is trying to become a learning organization.

One third of America's largest companies vanish every 15 years. That's a 33% fallout rate.

At the opposite end of the business spectrum, nine out of 10 start-ups fail within three years.

Like the rejects of natural selection it's all due to a failure to learn.

Can a company learn like a person?

If so, can we usefully apply our six step **M.A.S.T.E.R.** model of learning as an action plan to become a learning organization?

We think so — because it's not enough simply to become a learning organization, we need to become a *faster* learning organization. Better yet, a **M.A.S.T.E.R.** organization – where **your** personal development contributes to **our** corporate development.

Because the members of such a company need to think and act for themselves, there are a series of questions that we will need to think about on our way to becoming a Master Learning Organization.

Some of these questions are listed below, others will develop along the way. Some may raise issues we should have addressed before!

For each question there is an additional question "… and what shall we do about it?"

M.A.S.T.E.R.

M = Mind set
- What are the values we want in this company?
- Do we have the right physical conditions for learning faster?
- What rules do we want to see? (eg: no racial or sexual discrimination, family life must not be harmed by company hours.)
- How do we react to risk-taking and mistakes? Do we fix the blame or fix the problem? Is it safe to try something new – even if it fails?
- Are we uncomfortable about doing things the same way?
- Do we value novelty and excitement?
- Is learning recognized, celebrated and valued?
- What's the benefit to me, and my family, of us becoming a M.A.S.T.E.R. organization?
- What will I learn that will enhance my own employability?

A = Acquire the information
- How do we rate against our competition?
- What do our customers want? Who should know what I've found out about our market and how do I tell them?
- What **exactly** is my job? How does what I do contribute to our overall objectives? What's my main responsibility?
- What's the consequence of doing my job badly and/or outstandingly well?
- What could other people do to make it easier for me to do my job well?

S = Search out the meaning
- What vision for the organization can we all agree on? What are we trying to achieve? What would not just motivate me, but inspire me to work here?
- What's the gap between where we are now and where we want to be?
- How can we close it? What skills and knowledge will we need? Who in our company has got them? Can they teach those who need them? What other learning resources will we need? Books, videos, computer-based training, trainers?

- What will I learn? When? How? (That becomes my personal development plan.)
- How can we make each of our products or services better? Faster? More cost effective?
- How can we please the customer more?
- How can we become more efficient?
- Does everyone know how to learn and how to become a creative-analyst? (This book is a start!)
- What stops us achieving our goal? How can we remove these obstacles?

T = Trigger the memory
- How do we ensure that what we learn gets recorded and is available for reference by others, so we don't have to repeat the mistakes of history?

E = Exhibit what you know
- How do we spread information quickly and memorably and in such a way that people will act on it?
- Are we getting better at predicting the future?
- How will we know when we've succeeded in our aims?
- How can we reward learning and innovation? Should we reward people for highlighting problems? (You can't find solutions until you realize there is a problem.)
- Are we making more profit by being a learning organization? Is it all worth it?

R = Review the process
- How can we best ensure that the organization's goals, my personal goals and my family goals are each met? Is there a conflict between them?
- How can we go further? How can the concept of a M.A.S.T.E.R. organization be adapted to our families, to our local communities?
- How can we create a new style of organization that deliberately blurs the world of work, home and leisure? Do we want to?
- Are we making time to discuss our progress as a learning organization?
- Are we genuinely committed to the idea of a learning organization?

Note: These questions were developed with Sir Christopher Ball of Successful Learning

Increasing your employability

As we said at the start, the job you are doing now is unlikely to be the job you are doing in even three years' time.

In the world of work of the 21st century we will all need to train and retrain frequently and learn new skills every few years.

We will also need a new way of looking at work. New trends in work are emerging. Here are five of the most important. And they are good news for anyone who can learn fast and think well.

1 **You're the M.D.!**

More and more work is being done by small specialist companies working on contracts for larger companies. Even though you are working with us, try thinking of yourself as the Managing Director of your own one man or woman consultancy company – John Jones Ltd or Jane Jones Ltd – with a contract to do a job for us.

Thinking of yourself as an independent contractor highlights the need for you continuously to invest in the skills of your 'company,' so its value as a subcontractor keeps increasing.

If you are not continuously learning, you will be under-investing in your personal Research and Development Department. And if your skills are not up to date, your employability is reduced.

If you **are** investing in your own R&D continuously to upgrade your skills you'll be employable anywhere. That's true even if your present job changes or even ceases to exist.

2 **Focus on quality service**

To view yourself as 'independent' – contracting out your services – has important implications. It makes you ask questions like, "How can I service my customers better?" "How can I help them achieve their objectives?"

Customers aren't only outside the company. The people inside your company are also clients for your services. Do you give them a quality service?

Of course, they must approach their jobs the same way – looking for ways to help you do a better and better job.

Acting as if you were self-employed has another important implication. If something is wrong — fix it. Self-employed people don't waste time moaning about their company — they **are** the company! So they look for solutions and they move on to the next challenge.

"When they tell you to grow up, they mean stop growing."

Pablo Picasso

EMPLOYABILITY

"The era of womb-to-tomb employment is over.

The message for the smart worker is to learn as much as you can, about as much as you can, as fast as you can and increase your value to your employer, as well as your own career marketability."

Bud Carter,
The Executive Committee
Business Think Tank

"One of the hallmarks of the learning community is a system of principles that are shared and commonly understood among the members in the organization."

Mary Driscoll

If you are focused on providing a quality service, we need to focus on providing quality conditions. Quality must go both ways.

What ambitions do you have? How can the company help you fulfil those objectives? What will make the workplace pleasant and fulfilling for you?

We've seen that people learn best in a low threat, high energy environment. How can we create one?

3 **Look for continuous improvement**

The Japanese word 'kaizen' means a habit of mind that looks for continuous improvement. A daily quest to get better.

Sometimes a single heroic breakthrough, a new product or new way of doing things, produces a big improvement. The typical Japanese company, however, constantly searches for hundreds, even thousands, of small improvements. Each one may seem insignificant but accumulatively they add up to the difference between success and failure.

124 ways to cut costs

Here's a true story. A group of Japanese managers from a Yokohama steel mill was visiting a UK steel mill. Both mills had similar equipment of similar age, but the UK mill was losing money; the Japanese mill was making money.

At the end of the visit, the Chief Executive Officer of the UK steel mill turned to his visitors and said, "We have a lot to learn from you. What's the big difference? Why are you making money and we're not?"

Politely, the head of the Japanese delegation said tentatively, "Well, there isn't one big difference, but we do have one or two suggestions …". He then proceeded to list 124 ways the UK mill could improve! Here's a typical example.

When the three-foot blast-furnace doors opened to let a steel ingot roll out, the Japanese doors opened two inches less than the UK doors. So less heat was lost. It wasn't much, but over a year the saving on energy was appreciable. Added to the other 123 small differences, it was enough to turn a loss into a profit.

So the questions to ask every day are, "How can we do this better?" "How can we do this faster?" "How can we do this cheaper?"

These days we compete, not just with organizations within our own country, but on a global scale. And they are all asking the same questions.

That's why we are asking more of you – we simply have no choice. And that's why you have to ask more of yourself – because you are ultimately your own employer.

"Brainpower is becoming a company's most vital asset."

Michael J Marquardt
in Building The Learning Organization

The Japanese didn't invent kaizen. Most of the ideas came originally from the American management expert W Edwards Deming. But the Japanese added lots of small improvements to his original ideas!

If you are focused on continuous improvement to make the organization develop, the organization has to focus on helping you develop. Kaizen goes both ways.

As a learning organization we are interested in exploring how everyone can develop more of their potential. How can we assist your learning? How can we help your family learn? Can we buy self-study educational materials wholesale and pass on the benefits? Can we set up self-development courses that families can attend too? Work needs to be fulfilling.

Since no-one can predict the skills we will need in the future, it's in our mutual self interest for you to have as many skills as possible.

4   Embrace change

The stability of the past is gone. The only constant is accelerating change – in work practices, markets and technology. We simply have to keep up. We have to move fast, because our global competitors move fast. And we can't go fast if others go slow.

So there's no future in any of us resisting change, just because change is uncomfortable. If efficiencies can be made, they will be made – by someone. If it's not us, it will be another company. And that other company will ultimately offer the best job prospects.

The answer to change is not to resist it, but to learn to adapt to it. Even better, create the change ourselves. All of which is why we all need to be fast learners and creative-analysts.

The changes that all companies are having to ask of their employees are profound. Changes that once literally took centuries can happen in months. And that naturally makes all of us feel uncertain and nervous.

That's why we have introduced this programme and why we invite your family and your children to participate in it. In a fast changing world the core skills are learning and thinking.

5   Add value

An organization can only make a profit if the combined output of its employees exceeds its costs. Of course, wage costs are only a part of total costs. Other costs like raw materials and machinery and financial capital are big factors, too. But the cost you directly influence is your own.

"A century ago, a high school education was thought to be superfluous for factory workers and a college degree was the mark of an academic or a lawyer.

Now, for the first time in history, a majority of all new jobs will require university education."

William B Johnston and **Arnold H Packer** in Workforce 2000

RUST OUT

"The major problem facing the worker today is not 'burn-out' but 'rust-out.'

This is the result of a gross under-utilization of an individual's potential."

Dick Leider

"Lifelong learning and training is essential if our industry is to remain world-class."

Richard L Lesher, President of the US Chamber of Commerce

Jane Jones Ltd

"The whole workforce must be trained and it must be continuous training, not a little splat here and there, like an injection .... The old idea was that the schools cooked you until you were done, and then you went to work. Now, you've got to be constantly cooking."

Sue E Berryman,
Director of the National Center on Education and Employment

The people who are the most employable are the ones who contribute more to the company than they cost. The jargon for that is 'added value'.

That contribution isn't measured in the hours they put in or how busy they are. It can only be measured in whether they put in more than they take out.

So individuals also make an annual profit or loss – even if only companies officially report them.

That's why it is in everyone's self-interest to look constantly for ways to reduce the organization's expenses and increase our customers' satisfaction and sales. The higher the added value per employee in our company, the more secure your own job and earnings.

For example, the average added value per worker in the UK electronics industry in 1996 was £53,000, ie: the average worker added £53,000 more than they cost in salary + benefits + health insurance, etc.

In the top 10% of electronics companies, the average value added was £108,000. People working in those top 10% have a better job and income security.

If you are working to add value to the company and using new technology to increase efficiency, we must add value to you! Adding value also goes both ways.

That's why we will re-invest some of the rewards from efficiencies in education and training. That means you and your colleagues are fully equipped to master the skills that the new types of jobs will demand.

You'll see that becoming a learning organization will be pretty challenging! But it will be exciting and rewarding too.

Above all you will gain skills that will stand you in good stead in the fast-moving times ahead of us.

YOUR NOTES

"Active reading is a conversation with the author."
Consequently we invite you to use this page for notes and to ask yourself at least some of these questions.

What was the big idea? What was new?

What assumptions were made? Do I agree with them?

What was fact? Was the evidence reasonable? What was not clear?

What was opinion? Can I accept it? Was any issue oversimplified?

What are my main conclusions? What are the consequences?

How can I use what I've learned?   For my personal learning?   Training?   At home?

What do I want to explore further?

ANALYTICAL THINKING

The two pictures below make an important point. The drawing on the left was made by someone who, like most of us, had  not had any artistic training. The picture on the right was made by the **same** 63 year old woman after less than three hours' training.

Everyone can draw quite well if they follow a few simple rules.

In the same way, few of us can think well without some simple rules. These sorts of rules don't restrict. They liberate you by giving you a structure that acts as a guide towards a quality result. Just as we've developed a simple structure for learning, so we have developed some structures for quality thinking.

We talk about 'thinking' but, in fact, there are two main branches of thinking – creative thinking and analytical thinking.

These two ways of thinking are not opposites, because they continuously overlap. For example, you need to think creatively to solve problems and you need to think analytically to decide which of several creative possibilities is the best.

You need to be skilled in both types of thought. You need to be a creative-analyst.

"You know, it makes a lot of sense, if you don't think about it!"
Dagwood The Strip Cartoon

"All the resources we need are in the mind."

Theodore Roosevelt

Creative thinking

Thinking for new ideas and products. Seeing a new pattern or a relationship between things that was not obvious before.

Finding new ways to express things. Combining existing ideas to produce a new and better one.

Analytical thinking

Submitting a situation, problem, subject or decision to a logical step-by-step and rigorous examination.

Testing statements or evidence or proposals against objective standards. Seeing below the surface to the root cause of situations. Judging and deciding on a logical basis and detecting bias.

Thinking plus learning are the new natural resources, the new fountains of wealth.

As we said at the start of this book, you have to out-learn, out-think and out-create your competitors. Companies have to mobilize every ounce of their collective intelligence by ensuring that quality thinking is spread throughout the organization.

Who are the giants of history? Creative-analysts like Da Vinci, Einstein, Newton, Darwin.

Who are succeeding today? Creative-analysts like Bill Gates, Richard Branson, Stephen Hawking.

Learning to think well as a creative-analyst takes a lot of practice and the discipline not to be impetuous, but to follow some rules. Which is why creative analysis is very well paid! Moreover the threats we face as a society are created by poor thinking and can only be solved by creative analysis.

Analysis is good detective work

A good way to define something can be to describe its opposite. The opposite of someone who is a good creative-analyst is:

unimaginative	illogical
inconsistent	superficial
unfair	unclear
prejudiced	easily manipulated
vague	biased
narrow-minded	inaccurate

Not a very desirable set of characteristics is it?

The one word I didn't use is 'emotional,' because, as we've seen, there's an emotional content to all thought. And, in fact, analytical thinking turns out to have the emotional satisfaction of high class detective work.

The rules for quality thinking consist of asking the right questions – and remembering to ask them consistently.

You use analytical thinking to make a decision, to solve a problem, and to analyze and judge a situation. Let's look at each in turn and use some easily remembered 'thinking tools.'

"Aristotle was famous for knowing everything. He taught that the brain exists merely to cool the blood and is not involved in the process of thinking.

This is true only of certain persons."

Will Cuppy

"Most people would die sooner than think; in fact they do so."

Bertrand Russell

Making decisions

The acronym A FAN DANCE is a vivid way to remember how to make rational decisions and solve problems.

'**A FAN**' is used to make decisions.
It stands for:

> **A** ssumptions?
> **F** or?
> **A** gainst?
> **N** ow what?

You'll find that **A FAN** is a valuable structure for 'cool' judgment!

A = Assumptions

What exactly am I trying to decide? What have I assumed? What have I taken for granted?

Do I need more information? What are the facts? What's implied here?

It is possible, indeed rather common, to build an argument that seems completely logical, but from an initial premise that's false. If you assume too much blood is the cause of illness, it's logical to use leeches.

If the start point is wrong the result will be wrong. The way to the top may be to climb the ladder of success, but not if it's leaning against the wrong wall.

Sometimes the danger is 'circular logic'. Freud suggested every basic motive was sexual. When his patients objected that their motive wasn't sexual, he said that they were victims of suppressed sexuality. You can always be right with circular logic!

The next two letters of the acronym remind you to look at a subject from at least two points of view: your own first belief and the opposing viewpoint.

F = For

What is the evidence for my opinion? Is it good? Is it a fact or a belief? How did I come to believe this? What are the reasons for my belief? How certain can I be this is true?

A = Against

What could be the argument against my point of view? Can I see this another way? What if my starting assumption was wrong? How would an opponent argue this?

N = Now what?

This reminds you that a more careful assessment of the argument may well produce a wiser final decision. It usually does.

Edward de Bono gives a classic example. A class of teenagers were asked if they thought it would be a good idea to be paid to go to school. Twenty-nine out of 30 students immediately gave an enthusiastic 'yes'.

He then proposed they use his equivalent thinking tool: Plus/Minus/Interesting (P.M.I.). It caused them to stop and think (eliminating impetuosity) and look at both sides of the argument.

On reflection, 28 out of 30 students thought it was a bad idea. The search for alternative viewpoints threw up negatives like: possible bullying, cuts in school budgets to finance the payments, etc.

Solving problems

The acronym **DANCE** stands for:

D efinition
A lternatives
N arrow down
C hoose and check consequences
E ffect – act on it

D = Definition

A problem well stated is a problem half solved. It's critical to define exactly what the problem is before you start.

There's no point in finding an imaginative solution to the wrong problem. There's no point in having the most efficient oil rig in history, if you're drilling in the wrong place.

Most problems can be defined by asking:

- What's our goal? What are we trying to achieve?
- What do we mean by …? Give me an example. How else could we express it?
- Is there anything else we need to know?
- What exactly is the problem? Is it what it appears to be on the surface?

A = Alternatives

How many ways could I solve the problem, ie: move towards my goal?

The secret is not to look for a way but several ways to reach the goal. As Linus Pauling said, "The best way to have a good idea is to have lots of ideas."

This is the point where analytical thinking and creative thinking meet, for you would use your creative thinking tools to generate possible alternative solutions.

N = Narrow down

As we'll see, creativity is best served if you are not trying to judge your ideas at the same time as you are having them. However, having generated a lot of alternative solutions, you now need to start weeding out the least efficient. This is where a clear starting definition is so important – it helps you discard the options that do not fit the criteria you set.

A good question to ask is, "Which of those possible solutions meet my original criteria?"

C = Choose and check consequences

Having narrowed down your alternatives you need to choose the ideal option by seeing which solution best meets the criteria you set. You might well test each possibility with the FAN tool. What's for and what's against each one.

Then you would check the consequences of the action you propose by asking:

What effect would this have?

If my conclusion is true – what else must be true?

E = Effect

This is a reminder that the purpose of thinking is action – otherwise it's purely an intellectual exercise. As Professor Arnold of Stanford University puts it, "The creative process does not end with an idea – it only starts with an idea." Thinking without action is daydreaming.

Indeed, what marks out the successful creative-analyst is the degree to which they persist in action. It was true of Alexander Graham Bell, who was told that there was no need for a telephone because no-one else had one.

It was true of the first Xerox photocopier, which was refused financial support for four years. And Columbus needed 14 years to persuade the Spanish court to back his voyage – and even then he ended up at a completely different destination!

Rollo May in the aptly titled book *The Courage to Create* observed that, "Commitment is healthiest when it is not without doubt, but in spite of doubt".

The Five Whys

An excellent example of the need to define the problem correctly is told by Doug Jones in *High Performance Teamwork*. It also illustrates the power of another thinking tool – 'The Five Whys'.

Charbroil Inc. operates foundries making moulded iron and steel parts. Their problem was an excessive scrap rate. They asked the line workers why there was so much scrap. The answer was, "The tracks are worn, so the moulds don't fit correctly. That results in bubbles and rough edges" – ie: scrap.

So $100,000 was invested in new tracks. But with no improvement. So they asked again.

Why 1: Why are we getting scrap? Answer: "Because the metal is not hot enough." (They also asked, "Why didn't you say so before?" and got the reply "Because you didn't ask!" A lesson here.)

Why 2: Why is the metal not hot enough? Answer: "Because the glow rods are burned out."

Why 3: Why are the glow rods burned out? Answer: "Because there is metal spilled on them."

Why 4: Why is there metal spilled on them? Answer: "Because the cleaning crew spills metal on them."

Why 5: (To the cleaning crew) Why do you spill metal on the glow rods? Answer: "We were not aware we were spilling it – and we didn't realize it was significant if we did. Besides, we are competing with the first shift crew to see who can clean the most furnaces. There's a bonus on it."

The so simple, but so rarely used trick, is to keep asking 'why' until you get to the ultimate reason. Often it's at least five 'whys' deep, hence the title.

In this case a group of people who were not apparently connected with production were having a powerful impact on quality and profits.

The solution was to train the cleaning crews at the same time as the line crews, so each person understood how the results of his job affected the others. And to reward the quality of cleaning not the speed of work.

The overall result was to cut the usage of glow rods down from 20 a week to one a week. At $100 a rod this saved $100,000 a year. It also cut scrap rates down from 10% to 2%, which saved over $500,000 a year.

The example is a classic because:

- It illustrates the power of what's called **Systems Thinking**. Examining why a problem arises in depth and how it connects to other problems.

- It illustrates the power of questioning. Questions are like searchlights. They are the tools of truth – which is why quality thinking is based on them.

Just as it's important to define what the real problem is, so it's important to define exactly what the goal is.

You won't hit a target that you can't see. On the other hand, if you draw a circle round a target, it's easier to hit. An accurately expressed goal narrows your focus on the real problem.

Most goals can be defined accurately by asking:

- What prevents the outcome I want from happening and why?

- What conditions will exist when the problem is resolved, ie: how will I know when I've reached my goal?

- Can we quantify these conditions, ie: establish precise criteria for success?

It's vital to be precise. Any action plan must meet the **S.M.A.R.T** criteria.

It must be **S**pecific, **M**easurable, **A**ttainable, **R**esourced and **T**imetabled.

Analyzing situations

Any thorough analysis of a subject would need to ask the following six questions. When you apply this depth of analysis you are showing determination to get at the truth.

The questions are:

A What's the **AIM** of my thinking?
B What's the **BIG** idea?
C Am I really **CLEAR** about this?
D Am I analysing this in **DEPTH**?
E From whose **EYES** is this viewed?
F What **FOLLOWS** from this?

You can remember the questions to ask with the mnemonic

A, B, C, D, E, F.

A What's the AIM of my thinking?

Questions to ask are:

- What exactly am I trying to achieve?
- Why are we doing this analysis?
- What's the precise question we are trying to answer?

B What's the BIG idea?

We suggested earlier that you need to establish the core idea of what you are learning, early on. Once you've grasped the essence of the subject everything else 'fits in' and makes sense. It's the same for analytical thinking.

Most fruitless arguments are provoked because the parties haven't agreed on the core idea, the central concept. They are looking for solutions to two different problems. Of course, this is another way of saying you have to start with a clear, specific definition.

C Am I really CLEAR about this?

Questions that uncover 'woolly' thinking are:

- What do you mean by …?
- Let me see if I understand. I think you mean …
- Give me an example or an analogy.
- What would the opposite look like? (We did that to pin down clear thinking.)
- How will we know when we've succeeded?

D Am I analyzing this in DEPTH?

The 'Five Whys' technique is thinking in depth.

Questions to ask are:

- Is this an unjustified generalization?
- Are we over-simplifying the issues?
- Are we merely labelling things and taking them at face value?
- Have we seen how things connect to each other? What assumptions are being made?
- What are we taking for granted?
- What has been left out?
- What's implied that may not be true?
- Do we need more information?

E From whose EYES is this viewed?

Everything that is written, **everything** that is said, is **always** biased by the author's or speaker's previous experience.

Someone's judgment depends on how they interpret their past experiences – which is what forms their beliefs. There is always some bias in any book or statement, however small.

A quality initiative will look different to the Managing Director and a line operator, because their perspectives are different.

Our beliefs and experience cause us to create snap judgments. We are all too quick to 'label' situations or people. And then the label we apply prevents us from looking deeper.

In other words we pre-judge – which derives from the same word as prejudice. Statistically, tall defendants are acquitted more often than short defendants. Overweight people are paid less than normal-weight people for equivalent jobs. And, of course, racial and religious labelling is the most common form of prejudice.

It's completely illogical, of course, but it stems from our human instinct to live in groups and the genetic urge to protect 'us' – the insiders – at the expense of 'them' – the outsiders.

All that goes on deep in the primitive and instinctual part of the brain. No wonder prejudice is so difficult to deal with.

The fact that all thinking starts from a point of view is crucial to analytical thinking. How can you hope to change someone's mind unless you understand their start point – 'where they are coming from'?

To understand someone's point of view also helps clarify your own. It switches you from an attitude of "This is how it is" to "This is how I see it".

"How I see it" admits the possibility of alternatives.

Because everything that's said or written is always from the author's point of view you need to be asking:

- Who wrote this, what does he have to gain?
- Where did the information come from? Is it reliable?
- Is this opinion generalized to masquerade as fact?
- How representative are the examples? Does it favour one point of view? How biased is it? (You know it is biased!)
- What else could explain this?
- What's been left out?
- Is there enough evidence for this? Is it credible?
  And crucially …
- Is this a fact or a belief?

This last question is a key one. There is nothing wrong with beliefs – we couldn't live without them. But we need to be aware of them, because they control our actions.

That's not so easy, because they are rarely expressed openly. They exist in our subconscious, often with strong feelings attached.

You can start to examine your own – or someone else's beliefs – by asking:

- How did we come to that conclusion?
- How do we know?
- Can we justify and defend this statement?
- Are we certain? Or do we merely suspect this is true?
- Have we ever tested this opinion?
- How did we come to feel this way?

When you are prepared to ask these kinds of questions of yourself, as well as others, you are being intellectually honest – because you are applying a consistent standard of truth.

"How did we come to feel this way?" is a particularly important question because it says that you can separate thoughts from feelings.

Reason and emotion are not opposites, they are complementary. Reason is the ability to observe and assess feelings. And what's the point of holding a belief that doesn't stand up to scrutiny?

The attention we have paid to the question "Whose point of view is influencing this?" underlines how important it is.

F What FOLLOWS from this?

Questions to ask are:

- If this is true, what else follows?
- What are the consequences of this?
- How can I interpret this?
- What are the implications of this?

A reminder of this six point checklist again is:

A - AIM. Why are we examining this?
B - BIG IDEA. Do we agree on the core idea?
C - CLEAR. What exactly does this mean?
D - DEPTH. Are we assuming too much?
E - EYES. Whose point of view and prejudice is influencing this? Someone's is!
F - FOLLOWS. What are the implications of this?

"Few people think more than two or three times a year; I have made an international reputation for myself by thinking once or twice a week."

George Bernard Shaw

Maps of reality

We've stressed that understanding other people's point of view is critical.

A useful way to understand other people's points of view is to appreciate that we all carry our own 'map of reality' inside our heads – our interpretation of what we see – which will always be different from how others see it.

It's a good phrase, because it's clear that a map of France is not France. It's just a representation of France. It's not the reality – it's a version of that reality. And the map is only as good as the map-maker.

In the early days of cartography, maps were very inaccurate. For example, the cartographers only sailed around Australia. So the first maps were not only inaccurate, they only showed the coastal area of Australia. There was no representation of the interior at all. The maps were, literally, superficial.

AUSTRALIA

Gradually, through exploration, new perspectives were created and the map of Australia became more accurate.

Now, through the new perspective of satellite pictures, the maps are very accurate. But they are still not the reality of Australia. They are not the sights, the sounds, the smells, the taste, the heat, the humour, the people.

A map is just one perspective. It may be pretty accurate, but it can never be the reality. You can never 'live' in someone else's head.

But we can try to make sure that our map of his or her reality is not superficial. We can hear a different point of view and ask, "What would account for that point of view?" and say to ourselves, "I can't just dismiss it. I need to understand it."

"You are what you think and not what you think you are."

"A great many people think they are thinking when they are merely rearranging their prejudices."

William James

I think the energy of the environmental movement probably stems as much from N.A.SA's pictures of our beautiful blue planet hanging silent, vulnerable and lonely in space, as from the statistics on how fast our resources are running out.

All of a sudden we could actually see we were one human race, 'trapped' on one common home. It was a new perspective.

Attitudes determine outcomes

High quality analytical thinking is not only about rules, though they help, it's also about attitudes.

Those attitudes can best be summed up by asking, "Am I willing to …?"

1   **Persevere**. Writing this section took a long time because I read over 3,000 pages of theory and advice on thinking. And then my aim was to summarize it all so it would become a usable and memorable checklist to structure high quality thinking in any circumstances.

2   **Admit doubt**. We can only view the world from our own eyes, coloured by our own beliefs and within the limit of our own knowledge. That means few things are certain.

    Science can prove few things for certain; it mainly proves what's not true.

    Admitting there's a limit to our certainty is the start of being fair-minded.

3   **Fight for reason**. Since thinking skills are rarely taught, too many judgments are based on emotional beliefs and 'gut feelings'. Ironically, this is especially common with the major issues. My country right or wrong is a good example. And how many mergers founder on the egos of the participants?

There is a biological reason for this. You'll remember that the limbic system is the emotional centre of the brain – the brain of the brain, as Brazilian researcher Luiz Machado calls it.

Evolution has created a 'fast track' in this area of the brain that enables us to react very quickly to perceived danger. Useful in the wild but less useful in a business meeting!

So information, in certain circumstances, never even reaches the neo-cortex or 'thinking' brain. We see or hear something and simply react, 'without thinking'. The limbic system doesn't process logic – instead it encourages snap decisions and emotional reactions. So it takes effort to slow down our reactions and let the logical brain work on the facts.

It takes courage to stand out against peer pressure which is based on prejudice and to look for opinions that can be justified by reason. It also takes courage to apply the same standards to yourself.

"For those who do not think, it is best at least to rearrange their prejudices once in a while."

Luther Burbank

PERSEVERANCE

The structures for making decisions, solving problems and analyzing situations really work.

But only if they become a habit strong enough to overcome the impulse for snap judgments and knee-jerk reactions which is part of our evolutionary make-up.

Snap reactions may have served us well in the threatening, primitive world we inhabited as hunter-gatherers. They don't serve us well in the complex society we now live in.

The only way to make rational thinking a habit is to take the time to subject situations and problems to the sorts of checklists we've proposed.

Carrying a reminder of these checklists might be a good start!

PARENT TIPS

Thinking goes on silently in your head. So unless you talk out loud about the way you are structuring your reasoning, your child has no model of logical thought to work from.

Good thinking does require structure. You might like to put the main tools of rational thinking that we have detailed onto post cards.

Try to introduce them one at a time and look for as many instances where you could use this tool over, say, a month to think logically. In that way you can gradually introduce your child to an effective structure for logical thinking.

Implications for schooling

Subjects are a vehicle for thinking as well as being bodies of knowledge. So, for example, Physics teaches analytical thinking and Art and Music are subjects requiring complex thinking.

All this implies that the structure of analytical thinking is understood and practised by every teacher and embedded in all the lessons. That will need significant changes in teacher training.

Clear thinking is not common because many of the simplistic mental models we build as young children persist into adulthood. These 'gut' impressions can override years of factual training.

A recent TV documentary was filmed in the gardens where science graduates from Massachusetts Institute of Technology had gathered immediately after their graduation ceremony. The interviewer pointed to a huge tree and asked, "How did that tree get so big? Where did its bulk come from?"

The science graduates – all from one of America's most prestigious universities – floundered as badly as most of us would. The majority of them said that the bulk came "from nutrients from the ground". "Then why isn't there a big hole in the ground?" countered the interviewer. Blank faces.

The answer, of course, is that most of the bulk of the tree comes from nitrogen extracted by the tree from the air.

But this correct answer which they had learned – simply didn't **feel** right. They persisted in the childlike feeling that you can't magic something out of thin air! Gut reaction triumphed over logic.

The price of rational thinking is eternal vigilance!

Millions of people have been killed by leaders manipulating their beliefs.

So of all the things we could teach in school, the ability to understand how beliefs are formed and the willingness to examine them rationally would seem to be one of the most important.

But do we teach these skills?

THE QUALITY OF OUR THINKING DETERMINES THE QUALITY OF OUR LIVES

Richard Paul of the Institute for Critical Thinking makes the profound point that all learning is through thinking. Which is why the acquisition of learning techniques must be linked to thinking techniques.

Richard Paul then poses a further challenge. If the quality of our lives is largely determined by the quality of our thinking, then one of the primary purposes of school should be to teach disciplined thinking via the subjects being studied.

Analytical Thinking

DEFINITION?
ALTERNATIVES?
NARROW DOWN
CHOOSE/CONSEQUENCES
EFFECT/ACT

QUESTIONS ARE TOOLS OF TRUTH

THE 5 WHYS

SYSTEMS THINKING

S.M.A.R.T. criteria

Assumptions?
For?
Against?
Now what?

PROBLEM SOLVING

ANALYTICAL

DECIDING

CHECKLIST

A = aim?
B = big idea?
C = clarity
D = depth?
E = 'eyes'? point of view? bias?
F = follow? consequences?

FORMED EARLY

MENTAL MODELS THINKING

...AND PERSIST!

ATTITUDES

PERSEVERE
ADMIT DOUBT
FIGHT FOR REASON

YOUR NOTES

"Active reading is a conversation with the author."
Consequently we invite you to use this page for notes and to ask yourself at least some of these questions.

What was the big idea? What was new?

What assumptions were made? Do I agree with them?

What was fact? Was the evidence reasonable? What was not clear?

What was opinion? Can I accept it? Was any issue oversimplified?

What are my main conclusions? What are the consequences?

How can I use what I've learned? For my personal learning? Training? At home?

What do I want to explore further?

CREATIVE THINKING

Can you plan to be creative? Absolutely. Creativity is not sitting around waiting for a flash of inspiration. There's always a good deal of hard work and preparation involved.

Beethoven drafted and redrafted his compositions dozens of times. What eventually became masterpieces started as ordinary, sometimes even uninspiring drafts.

A survey of authors confirms that the actual creative writing takes up a mere 20% of their time while research consumes about 40% and revision 40%. In other words, as Edison famously said, "Genius is 99% perspiration and 1% inspiration."

Of course, motivation helps too. When Handel was asked how he could have written a work as glorious as the Messiah in only 22 days, he said it was because he needed the money!

Start with (lots of) knowledge

Acquiring detailed background knowledge on the subject is a key to creativity – because almost all new ideas are simply a re-combination of existing ideas. The creative person always knows a lot about his subject.

The flash of inspiration comes from a background of expert knowledge.

So, the first rule of creative thinking is – do your homework. But facts alone are not enough. The advent of personal computers and the Internet means that there is no shortage of source material on any subject.

The creative prizes do not go to the people who can simply acquire facts. They go to the people who can manipulate those facts and combine them in new ways.

The creative attitude

Once you've steeped yourself in the subject you need a way to look at it from new angles.

Visit the Picasso museum in Barcelona and what strikes you is the years of practice he spent perfecting the art of conventional draughtsmanship.

He needed the foundation of technical ability before he could progress towards his innovations. Even then he sketched many versions before creating his final masterpieces.

WHAT'S ALREADY KNOWN?

Isaac Newton, one of the most creative scientists of all time, summed up the importance of wide background knowledge when he said:

"If I have been able to see further than others, it is because I have stood on the shoulders of giants."

Picasso once said, "Every act of creation is first of all an act of destruction." He meant you need to break out of the conventional ways of looking at things. A work of art is one that gives a new perspective or captures a new trend in society.

It follows that creativity also needs courage. If you are escaping from conventional ways of thinking, you are involved in risk. The fruit of the tree may be out on a limb – but it takes courage to crawl out there and grasp it.

It's hard to break out of conventional ways of thought because we need to be on automatic pilot much of the time. Life would simply be too challenging if – each day – we had to work out afresh how to shave, dress, make breakfast, or work.

The mind labels activities as routine, and then places all similar events in the same category. But this habit of labelling means that, once the label has been applied, thinking becomes rigid, conventional.

That's why young children are more creative than adults. Their minds are still finding patterns in behaviour and their labels are not yet strong enough to restrict their thinking.

Unfortunately, the over-emphasis on the single right answer in schools starts to diminish that creativity. As Neil Postman says in *Teaching is a Subversive Activity*, "Children enter school as question marks and leave as full stops".

The three stages of creation

Robert Sternberg of Yale University has extensively researched creativity. He sees three stages.

Insight
You define the problem carefully and sift the relevant data from the irrelevant. Like a detective, you decide which clues are important.

Combination
You re-combine ideas in a new way. When Charles Darwin produced his theory of evolution, all the information had been known for years. His talent was to combine old ideas into a new concept.

Compare old and new
You can't see the value of the new idea unless you compare it to the old, which takes time and patience. So creativity needs perseverance.

All this is very encouraging because it shows that there is a common pattern in all creativity – a framework. So it puts creativity within the reach of us all. Follow the plan and you can think creatively.

Methodical creativity!

Giotto's 1305 fresco of the Virgin and Christ is a work of art because it was the first painting to attempt a three dimensional effect.

Albrecht Durer's painting The Young Hare (1502) is a work of art because it was the first time an artist had tried to paint an object exactly as he saw it, correct in every detail. Now colour photography means such an approach would no longer automatically qualify it as a work of art.

AVOID LABELS

When engineer William Gordon was given the job of creating a new way to open cans, he showed how to avoid the rigid thinking caused by 'labelling.'

When he briefed his group of engineers he deliberately did not use the word 'can opener'. Otherwise, they would have had a conventional picture in their heads before they started.

Because they were not inhibited by this 'label', they were able to discuss other ways of getting at the inside of things.

They looked for analogies and someone suggested that a banana was easy to open because you 'unzipped' the skin.

The ring pull can was born.

Creativity risks failure and almost certain criticism.

Robert Louis Stevenson (who set out to create the plots of his novels in his dreams) requested, "Give me the young man who has brains enough to make a fool of himself".

The framework for creativity

We began with the premise that you can plan to be creative, so let's look at the tools for 'methodical creativity.' We can say, "It's **A FARCE**".

A Amass – lots of information
F Four-way thinking – look at it from all angles
A Alternatives – generate lots of ideas
R Re-combine – look for the best combinations of these ideas
C Choose – decide on the best combination
E Effect – put it into action.

A = Amass

Very few important breakthroughs are made by amateurs. You need to be steeped in the subject. So do your research.

F = Four-way thinking

The way to break out of rigid thinking is to look at the problem from different directions. We call it four-way thinking and it's explained on pages 144 - 145.

A = Alternatives

"The best way to have a good idea is to have lots of ideas."

An outcome of our educational system is that we become used to looking for the **one** correct answer. In the real world there are usually several possible answers. If you stop looking – after finding an answer that fits – you will often miss a much better answer.

The question to ask is, "How **many** ways could we find to answer this problem? Let's find at least 10".

Robert Olsen, in *The Art of Creative Thinking*, explains why insisting on quantity works. If you simply ask people to list 'some' birds they will start with obvious examples – sparrows, pigeons, blackbirds, etc.

If, however, you force them to produce a specific quantity – 30, for example – they eventually start thinking in categories. So thinking of a turkey leads to other domestic birds – chickens, ducks and pheasants. And a seagull leads to albatross, kitty hawk, puffin and skua.

Suddenly the obvious starts to become the unusual. By forcing quantity we can lead the brain into new and creative areas.

The other reason that sheer quantity is important is that many ideas are actually not much good! They are still important though, because they may lead to eventual success. You don't have to be right at each stage in creative thinking – only at the end.

So even apparently silly ideas can be the all-important stepping stone to a breakthrough. It's like gold mining. You have to dig up five tons of ore to produce one ounce of gold.

A good technique for creating lots of alternative ideas is brainstorming – examined on pages 146 - 147.

R = Re-combine

Creating an armoury of alternative ideas rarely produces a breakthrough by itself. Usually you need to combine a number of these new ideas.

Gordon Dryden is a creativity expert and has created an excellent training programme to teach creativity which he calls *The Ah Ha Game*.

He defines an idea as 'a new combination of old elements'. "There's nothing new under the sun," he says, "there are only new combinations of old elements".

"Recipes in cookbooks," says Dryden, "are merely new combinations of existing ingredients". Every man-made fibre is a new combination of existing atoms.

A fax combines a copying machine and a telephone. The Gutenberg press combined a die for making coins with a press for making wine.

So once you have generated plenty of alternatives, you then ask yourself, "What can I combine to get a good answer?" (NB: not **the** only answer.)

Learning maps are again useful. Since the ideas are all on one page, it's easier to see the potential combinations.

C = Choose and consequences

Out of all these new ideas, what's the best idea?

Which idea best meets the criteria we initially set? What would be the consequence of choosing it?

E = Effect

Now put the best idea to work, otherwise it's all impractical daydreaming.

You'll note the last two elements in our creative thinking plan are **Choose (C)** and **Effect (E)**. They are exactly the same as for problem solving.

That's because it's here that Creative Thinking gives way to Analytical Thinking, in order to decide on the best course of action.

Four-way Thinking

TOP-DOWN
create an overview

FRONT-TO-BACK
work forwards

BACK-TO-FRONT
work backwards

BOTTOM-UP
upside down

1 FRONT-TO-BACK THINKING

This is our normal approach, which we've examined in Analytical Thinking. It starts with the problem and works step-by-step towards a solution. To remind you, the steps are:

D Define the problem – which must be the start point of all thinking
A Generate lots of alternatives
N Narrow down the alternatives
C Choose one and check for the consequences
E Put into action – effect

2 BACK-TO-FRONT THINKING

Here you start with the solution and work backwards to see how it might have come about.

Here's an example. An architect designed a new building complex that surrounded a large square area. The square was to be seeded with grass. The landscape gardener asked where the paths should be built in the quadrangle.

The architect's answer was, "Seed the whole area with grass and wait a year". Sure enough, during the year the natural traffic flow of people between buildings marked out the most frequent routes, which were then officially paved.

Good back-to-front questions to ask are:

What is standing in the way of the solution I want? What's the simplest way of removing those obstacles? The word 'simplest' is important. Scientists look for elegant, ie simple solutions.

A good example of elegant back-to-front thinking comes from pest control. The problem was how to get rid of tsetse flies. Front-to-back thinking would look for ways to kill them.

Back-to-front thinking said, 'Suppose they didn't exist, how might that come about?'

The answer is they were never born. From that insight came a solution. Release insects with a modified gene that causes sterility in the offspring so that they would gradually die out.

3 BOTTOM-UP THINKING

This way of thinking asks you to turn the problem upside down. A child sees the world differently when he bends down and peers through his legs.

Edward Jenner had the inspiration to switch from asking why people got smallpox to asking why dairy maids did not get smallpox. In so doing he discovered that they were exposed to a very mild form of cowpox which 'immunized' them from getting the more serious smallpox.

So was born the idea that you can protect people from infectious diseases by inoculating them with a minute amount of the original disease. This triggers the immune system to activate a strong defence against a real attack.

Edward de Bono supplies an amusing example of reverse or upside-down thinking. There are 120 entrants for a knock-out tennis tournament. How many matches must be played, including byes, to produce the winner?

To work out the answer with logic is time consuming. But turn the question upside down – shift your perspective – and the answer comes in a second.

So, instead of concentrating on the winner, ask instead how many losers are there? If 120 players start there must be 119 losers. Each loser plays once, including byes. So there must be 119 matches.

Think 'out of the box'

Henry Ford employed 'upside-down thinking' when he invented the assembly line and moved the work past the worker, not the worker to the work. Today, we are moving the office to the worker (the electronic cottage) not the worker to the office.

A good question to ask is, "How could we express this in a completely different way?"

When "How can we train our people better?" becomes "How can they learn what they need to know?" you shift from top-down corporate training to bottom-up self-directed learning – which is the basis of the learning organization.

When you turn the question, "How can we cure sickness better?" upside down, and rephrase it into, "How can we help people to stay well?" you focus on the common denominators of people who stay healthy into old age. You start to draw some significant conclusions on the role of nutrition and stress control.

Humour can kick-start creativity. Two shoe salesmen were dispatched to an undeveloped country. One faxed back, "No opportunity here – no-one wears shoes". The other faxed back, "Fabulous opportunity – no-one wears shoes".

Bottom-up thinkers see challenging opportunities. Conventional thinkers see problems.

4   TOP-DOWN THINKING

Top-down thinking reminds us of the importance of an overview. It's especially important in resolving problems involving people. And when you are personally involved.

This way of thinking asks you to imagine that you are looking at the situation from above, seeing yourself as just one of the participants. All of a sudden you become more objective, a fly on the ceiling, and more ready to see other people's viewpoints.

Chess is a good example of top-down thinking – you cannot play the game unless you also see your opponent's viewpoint and therefore possible moves.

Top-down thinking is an essential element in any negotiation. If you don't take an overview, you will only pursue the deal from your own perspective, and lose the chance of a win/win solution.

Stand away to see clearly

There's an Eastern saying – "We can only control those things that we have stood away from". It is part of the art of letting go. When anger or jealousy or regret lives inside us, it feeds on us and drains our attention and energy.

To overcome destructive emotions requires that we can say, "I am feeling anger at the moment, but I am not controlled by this anger" or "I have failed at this particular task, but I am not a failure".

You cannot learn to understand yourself or others, unless you achieve the ability to be detached.

However, to look at yourself and others from outside your emotions doesn't mean you are cold or emotionless. It is a temporary adjustment you need to make to give you a clearer perspective, before you then re-engage your emotional self.

It's rather like a painter who stands back from his canvas to judge it better.

Top-down thinking is most necessary when you feel strongly that you are right!

Good questions to ask would be:

- How would a detached observer see this?
- How does this specific problem connect with the subject as a whole?
- Is this merely a symptom of a bigger problem?

Top-down thinking is to creativity what systems thinking is for analysis. A way to ensure that you don't focus on a detail and miss its relationship to the big picture.

"Chance favours the prepared mind."

Louis Pasteur

Brainstorming

Brainstorming is a 'structured free-for-all,' popularized by adman Alex Osborn. The aim is to generate as many ideas as possible within the following rules.

1 Everyone is well briefed on the facts.

2 The more unusual the ideas the better.

3 Everyone must have a turn (no-one dominates).

4 The more ideas the better.

5 No-one may criticize any idea.

This is the key rule. You need these stepping stones. If you allow the more analytical left brain to interfere at this stage, you will curb the creative flow. The time to judge or criticize is after you've created a large pool of ideas.

6 Deliberately seek combinations of ideas.

7 Ensure someone monitors the discussion to see that it stays focused and relevant to the problem.

A good way to keep track of the ideas would be on a learning map. Because they are all on one visual map, it makes it easier to see how separate ideas could be connected.

A checklist to keep the ideas flowing is through the use of yet another acronym – **C.A.S.P.A.R**.

It's not a friendly ghost but a friendly checklist to remind you to ask the key 'what if' questions that trigger alternative ideas. It stands for:

C **Cut out** – What can we eliminate or replace?

A **Add** – What can we add/increase or make longer?

S **Subtract** – What can we reduce/decrease or make shorter?

P **Put** to another use – What else could we use this for?

A **Adapt** – What else is similar? What analogies help?

R **Rearrange** – Can we reverse or alter the existing order?

Let's look at some examples. The point is not to create a finished idea, but to start the process of thought. Remember the key rule for brain-storming

is to avoid criticizing ideas straight away, but to use 'what if' type thoughts as stepping stones to the ultimate new idea.

CUT OUT
- What if we eliminated income tax and instead introduced a minimum wage? But we also increased the sales tax on everything except food, educational material and children's clothes?
- What if we replaced the habit of routine thinking, with the habit of asking, 'What if?'

ADD
- What if we increased the amount of school time for art, drama and music (and thinking and learning skills)?
- What if company employees were given thinking skills training? Would you get a workforce that needed less supervision?
- What if you knew you could add 20 years to your expected lifespan and live to 110? What difference would it make to how you plan your life? (It's likely to become true.)

SUBTRACT
- What if we reduced the number of secondary school teachers and added more interactive computers?
- What if we reduced prison sentences, but made the guilty parties work directly for the victim?

PUT TO ANOTHER USE
- What if retired people became mentors to the company's new recruits?
- What if every country's defence department had to be staffed by women? Would international aggression be cut?

ADAPT
- What if we adapted an oil drill as a domestic tool? (It's called a power drill.)
- What if museums became teachers? (The best already have, like the Exploratorium in San Francisco, or the Science and Natural History museums in London.)

The 'adapt' part of the checklist is an excellent place to look for analogies – comparing a familiar situation with the problem you are trying to solve or the subject you are trying to understand.

The Wright Brothers used analogous thinking to work out how to manoeuvre a plane. They watched buzzards and noticed how the birds not only dropped a wing to turn but also twisted their wing. The extra pressure levelled the bird off. That analogy produced a wing tip that could be separately manoeuvred – an aileron.

Analogies work because they help create a new perspective. In the words of Dr William Gordon of the Synectics Corporation (who developed the ring pull can), "They help to make the familiar strange".

This is necessary, he says, because our inclination is always to oversimplify things to make them familiar. Analogies force us to look afresh and promote creativity.

A good question to ask is, "What is this like? What can I learn from the comparison?"

REARRANGE

- What if classes were composed of students who had reached the same level in the subject – instead of arranging the class by age?

- What if corporate trainers became learning advisers to individual members of staff – working out a separate training plan for each person that met his or her personal needs?

CAUTION!

Don't brainstorm for alternative ideas and then try to come up with the final idea all in one day. Study after study of creativity has shown that you are better switching off and letting your subconscious mind work on the problem.

So review your ideas during the evening and focus on the outcome that you want. This gives your subconscious a specific goal to work to.

Then sleep on it. Beethoven, Wagner, Coleridge and Robert Louis Stevenson all deliberately used dreams as a source of creative ideas.

The result, so very often, is a flash of inspiration. But note it comes from a very well prepared mind indeed. This wasn't a chance flash of inspiration, it came from 'methodical creativity'.

Beethoven, asked where his ideas for composition came from, said, "They come to me in the silence of the night or in the early morning, stirred into being by moods".

Goethe walked in order to get ideas. Rousseau also did his best thinking on walking trips alone. Nietzsche listened to music in the evening and awoke full of "resolute insights and inspirations".

NEW COMBINATIONS OF OLD IDEAS

The common thread in all creativity is the combination of old elements in new ways. A multiplex cinema is a creative idea, so is the Sony Walkman.

Every book written in English is made up of words that are composed from only 26 letters. Everything in the world is a recombination of atoms of which there are only about 100 different types.

We humans are made from chemical elements that come from our planet. Carbon, oxygen, hydrogen, sodium, calcium, potassium, phosphorous, copper, zinc, etc. In all about $36 worth of materials – which definitely makes the whole worth more than the sum of its parts.

In turn, as astronomer Carl Sagan points out, our planet and our bodies are created from the debris from some long distant stellar explosion.

We are all made of 'star stuff'. We are all space men and women.

We are all made of star stuff

Thinking skills are learnable

We believe that the key to the fast-moving and complex world of the 21st century is to learn fast and to become a high quality creative-analyst. **Both talents are learnable.**

Both analysis and creativity need to be methodical. It might, therefore, be a good idea to copy down on four post cards the acronyms we've suggested and commit them to memory in the same way as **M.A.S.T.E.R.** gives you a checklist for learning.

A FAN	for decision making
DANCE	for problem solving
A,B,C,D,E,F	for analyzing situations
A FARCE	for creativity (including **C.A.S.P.A.R.** for brain storming alternatives)

Of course, thinking cannot be done in the abstract. You need a particular subject or problem to work on. So you may memorize the checklists but you cannot become a good thinker without applying these thinking tools over and over and over, until they become an automatic way of thinking.

Henry Mintzberg of the McGill University Faculty of Management extensively studied corporate executives.

He concluded that, "Organizational effectiveness does not lie in that narrow-minded concept called 'rationality'; it lies in a blend of clear-headed logic and powerful intuition".

"Genius is seeing what everyone has seen, and thinking what no-one has thought."

Albert Saint-Gyorgi
Discoverer of Vitamin C

"Thinking is the hardest work of all. That's why so few people do it."

Henry Ford

PARENT TIPS

These two sessions on the acquisition of thinking skills can be neatly summarized by Henry Ford's famous observation; quoted on the previous page.

What lessons are to be learned for the education of our children?

Says Philip Goldberg, author of *The Intuitive Edge*, "We should convey to students a greater respect for their innate capacity for fantasy, visualization and imagination, all of which aid intuition.

We would make great progress toward liberating the child's intuitive abilities if we placed more emphasis on personal discovery rather than rote memorization of facts or the mechanical application of rules for problem-solving.

In most educational settings, students are given problems rather than being allowed to find their own. Then they are told what form the expected answer is to take and asked to follow prescribed procedures to get there.

It would be far better if, at least on occasion, they were allowed to experience first-hand what we all have to do in adulthood: identify problems concerning matters we care about and find our own ways of solving them."

One of the most important models you can provide for your child is continuous wonder.

"I wonder how they make cornflakes?"

"Where does the water go when we flush the loo?"

"Why does water expand when it freezes, when most other things get smaller?"

"What would happen if we put sugar in washing-up liquid – would it make bigger bubbles?"

"Why does vinegar make coins shiny?"

"What if money grew on trees and everyone could pick off as much as they wanted?"

"What would it be like to be as small as a mouse?"

"What if the sun never set?"

"There is no expedient to which a man will not go to avoid the real labour of thinking."

Thomas Alva Edison

THINKING PAYS

"Wealth is the product of man's capacity to think."
Ayn Rand

Curiosity is fundamental to creativity. Nature programmed your child to be curious and creative. Don't let our false quest for the one true answer drain it out of her.

Creative Thinking

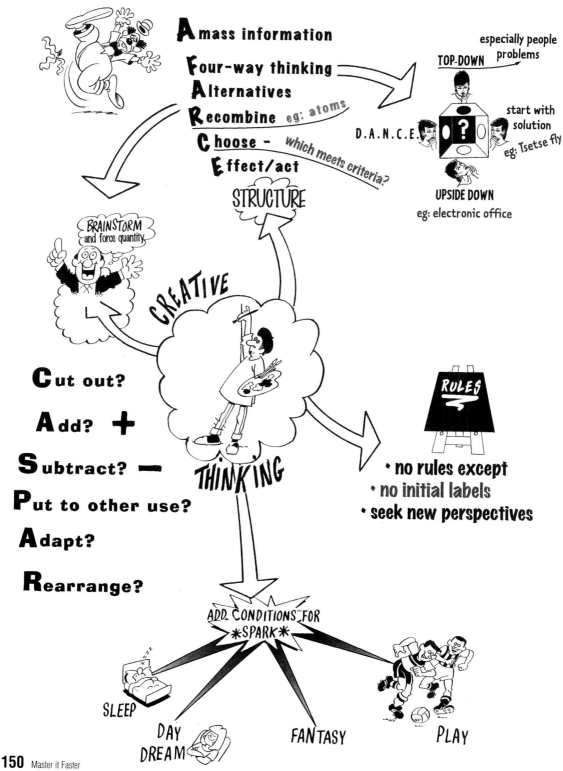

Amass information

Four-way thinking

Alternatives

Recombine *eg: atoms*

Choose – *which meets criteria?*

Effect/act

especially people problems

TOP-DOWN

D.A.N.C.E.

start with solution
eg: Tsetse fly

UPSIDE DOWN
eg: electronic office

STRUCTURE

BRAINSTORM
and force quantity

CREATIVE

THINKING

Cut out?

Add? +

Subtract? —

Put to other use?

Adapt?

Rearrange?

RULES

• no rules except
• no initial labels
• seek new perspectives

ADD CONDITIONS FOR
✳SPARK✳

SLEEP

DAY
DREAM

FANTASY

PLAY

YOUR NOTES

"Active reading is a conversation with the author."
Consequently we invite you to use this page for notes and to ask yourself at least some of these questions.

What was the big idea? What was new?

What assumptions were made? Do I agree with them?

What was fact? Was the evidence reasonable? What was not clear?

What was opinion? Can I accept it? Was any issue oversimplified?

What are my main conclusions? What are the consequences?

How can I use what I've learned?   For my personal learning?   Training?   At home?

What do I want to explore further?

Suggested reading

Armstrong, T (Ph.D.) 1993. *7 Kinds of Smart*. N.Y., Penguin Books.

Beck, Joan B, and Sternberg, Robert J 1986. *How to Raise a Brighter Child*. N.Y., Pocket Books.

Borysenko, J (Ph.D.) 1988. *Minding The Body, Mending The Mind*. London, Bantam.

Buzan, Tony 1993. *The Mind Map Book*. N.Y., Dutton.

Costa, Arthur L 1991. *Developing Minds: A Resource Book for Teaching Thinking*. Revised Edition, Vol. 1. Alexandria VA, ASCD.

Csikzentmihalyi, M 1990. *Flow: The Psychology of Optimal Experience*. N.Y., Harper & Row.

De Bono, Edward 1970. *Lateral Thinking: Creativity Step-by-Step*. N.Y., Harper & Row.

Dryden, Gordon and Vos, Jeannette. 1994. *The Learning Revolution*. Rolling Hills CA, Jalmar Press.

Gardner, H 1985. *Frames of Mind. The Theory of Multiple Intelligences*. N.Y., Basic Books, Inc.

Gardner, H 1993. *Multiple Intelligence: The Theory in Practice*. N.Y., Basic Books.

Goleman, Daniel. 1995. *Emotional Intelligence*. N.Y., Bantam Books.

Handy, C 1989. *The Age of Unreason*. London, Century Hutchinson.

Houston, J 1982. *The Possible Human: A Course in Enhancing Your Physical, Mental and Creative Abilities*. L.A., Tarcher.

Johnson, D, and Johnson, R 1990. *Learning Together and Alone*. Englewood Cliffs NJ, Prentice-Hall.

Kline, Peter, and Saunders, Bernard. 1993. *Ten Steps to a Learning Organization*. Arlington VA, Great Ocean Publishers.

May, Rollo. 1975. *The Courage to Create*. N.Y., W.W. Norton.

Nickerson, Raymond S, Perkins, David N, and Smith, Edward E 1985. *The Teaching of Thinking*. Hillsdale NJ, Lawrence Erlbaum Associates.

Parnes, Sidney J 1981. *The Magic of Your Mind*. N.Y., Bearly Ltd.

Paul, Richard W 1990. *Critical Thinking: What Every Person Needs to Survive in a Rapidly Changing World*. Santa Rosa CA, Foundation for Critical Thinking.

Perkins, David. 1995. *The Mind's Best Work*. Cambridge MA, Harvard University Press.

Pike, Robert W 1990. *Creative Training Techniques Handbook*. Minneapolis MN, Lakewood Books.

Rico, GL 1983. *Writing The Natural Way: Using Right Brained Techniques to Release Your Expressive Power*. L.A., Tarcher.

Rose, Colin and Nicholl, Malcolm. 1998. *Accelerated Learning for the 21st Century*. London, Piatkus.

Senge, Peter M 1990. *The Fifth Discipline: The Art and Practice of the Learning Organization*. N.Y., Doubleday.

Tobin, Daniel R 1993. *Re-Educating the Corporation: Foundations for the Learning Organization*. Essex Junction VT, Oliver Wright Publications.

Tracy, Brian. 1993. *Maximum Achievement*. N.Y., Simon & Schuster.

Wick, Calhoun W, and Leon, Stanton Lu 1993. *The Learning Edge: How Smart Managers and Smart Companies Stay Ahead*. N.Y., Prentice Hall.

L.A. = Los Angeles   N.Y. = New York

Other programmes from Accelerated Learning Systems

If you have enjoyed *Master it Faster* you may like to explore these other products.

FRENCH, SPANISH, GERMAN, Italian for English speakers, and ENGLISH for Japanese speakers through HOME STUDY.

Courses include video and audio cassettes, text books, games and memory maps. Everything you need to learn a new language – quickly, enjoyably and effectively. Used extensively and successfully by many leading organizations.

FUNDAMENTALS

A development programme for pre-school children age 0-6 years old. Helps parents create a rich, stimulating home environment to build brain capacity and rounded abilities. Supported by leading educators.

YES, YOU CAN...DRAW

A first stage drawing course available as a video and workbook.

For details please contact:

Accelerated Learning Systems Ltd, 50 Aylesbury Road, Aston Clinton, Aylesbury, Bucks, UK. HP22 5AH.
Tel: 01296 631177 Fax: 01296 631074
email: colinrose@globalnet.co.uk
web: www.accelerated-learning-uk.co.uk